Cambridge Elements ≡

Elements in Applied Social Psychology
edited by
Susan Clayton
College of Wooster, Ohio

T0329137

LEARNING FROM VIDEO GAMES (AND EVERYTHING ELSE)

The General Learning Model

Douglas A. Gentile
Iowa State University

J. Ronald Gentile
State University of New York, Buffalo

CAMBRIDGE
UNIVERSITY PRESS

CAMBRIDGE
UNIVERSITY PRESS

University Printing House, Cambridge CB2 8BS, United Kingdom

One Liberty Plaza, 20th Floor, New York, NY 10006, USA

477 Williamstown Road, Port Melbourne, VIC 3207, Australia

314–321, 3rd Floor, Plot 3, Splendor Forum, Jasola District Centre, New Delhi – 110025, India

103 Penang Road, #05–06/07, Visioncrest Commercial, Singapore 238467

Cambridge University Press is part of the University of Cambridge.

It furthers the University's mission by disseminating knowledge in the pursuit of education, learning, and research at the highest international levels of excellence.

www.cambridge.org
Information on this title: www.cambridge.org/9781108965934
DOI: 10.1017/9781108966511

First published 2021

A catalogue record for this publication is available from the British Library.

ISBN 978-1-108-96593-4 Paperback
ISSN 2631-777X (online)
ISSN 2631-7761 (print)

Learning from Video Games (and Everything Else)

The General Learning Model

Elements in Applied Social Psychology

DOI: 10.1017/9781108966511
First published online: December 2021

Douglas A. Gentile
Iowa State University

J. Ronald Gentile
State University of New York, Buffalo

Author for correspondence: Douglas A. Gentile, dgentile@iastate.edu

Abstract: Video games can have many effects on players, some of which could be intentional effects (e.g., games designed to train health compliance behaviors), and most of which are unintentional (e.g., violent games, stereotypes, gaming disorder). Some of these areas of research have been seen as controversial, but many of the controversies can be at least partially resolved by considering the learning mechanisms underlying the effects. We describe the General Learning Model in greater detail than has been provided elsewhere, including short-term and long-term mechanisms, processes of learning and forgetting, and moderators of learning. Video games use many of the best practices to train for both mastery and for transfer of learning. The implications for re-interpreting the literature on violent video games and gaming disorder, as well as for applied social psychology broadly defined, are discussed.

Keywords: General Learning Model, gaming disorder, learning mechanisms, prosocial video games, violent video games

ISBNs: 9781108965934 (PB), 9781108966511 (OC)
ISSNs: 2631-777X (online), 2631-7761 (print)

Contents

1 Introduction

If you'll permit me (Doug) to reminisce before we get to the science, I've had a long relationship with video games, starting in 1973 when I became mesmerized by *Pong*'s bluish-white blip of light moving back and forth across the screen. By the late 1970s, games like *Space Invaders* and *Asteroids* captured a lot of my quarters. In 1980, my high school got a Commodore PET personal computer – one for the whole school. It lived in the algebra classroom, mostly collecting dust until John Wood and I began to stay after school several days a week to teach ourselves the BASIC computer language. And what did we code? Games, of course. Some were simple logic-based games and others were strategy based, similar to the *Hammurabi* game – a text-based strategy game where you make decisions about land and resource use to feed your people while dealing with random problems like drought.

Our games weren't very sophisticated, clever, or complex. The PET only had 16 kilobytes (not megabytes, not gigabytes, but kilobytes!) of memory, and we often found ourselves bumping up against this hard limit when trying to write our programs. Nonetheless, most of the fun for us was in the writing and testing of code.

In college, I purchased a Commodore 64 personal computer – oh, the freedom of 64 kilobytes of memory (again, not megs, not gigs)! Who would ever need that much? It turns out I did. I created and coded a sprawling "dungeons and dragons"-type of text-based adventure game that used every bit of it. My brother Chris would visit, and we would play all day.

After college, I worked at Educational Testing Service as a statistical computer programmer, writing in Fortran 7 on mainframe computers. These computers included a copy of the ELIZA program – a text-based program designed to interact with you similarly to how a Rogerian psychotherapist might (see Figure 1; Hall, 2019).

Although not designed as a game, per se, it was fun to try to mess with ELIZA's language parsing and limited ability to handle non sequiturs. Here is a conversation I recently had with her:

> Hello, I am Eliza.
* Hello Eliza. I'm hungry.
> How long have you been hungry?
* Since I saw your blue blue eyes.
> Why are you concerned about my blue blue eyes?
* I feel that they have a grip on my soul and you're never going to let go.
> Does it please you to believe I am never going to let go?
* Yeah, sure. I'm sick of being responsible for my own life.
> Do you believe it is normal to be sick of being responsible for your own life?

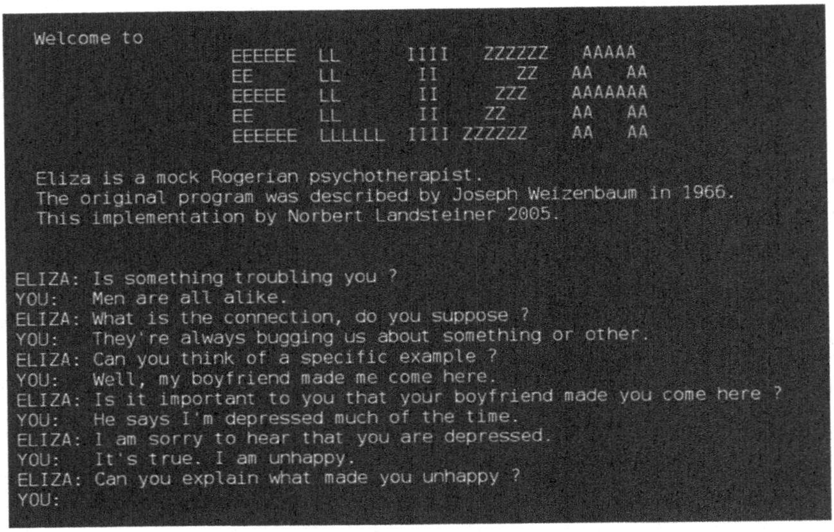

Applied Social Psychology

Figure 1 Eliza demonstration (from https://en.wikipedia.org/wiki/ELIZA)

* Who is to say what's normal and what isn't?
> Does that question interest you?
* Well, I AM a psychologist. Unlike you.
> Do you enjoy being a psychologist? Unlike me?

You can talk to her yourself at http://psych.fullerton.edu/mbirnbaum/ psych101/Eliza.htm.

In 1992, however, I got a completely new view on the power of games to interact with human psychology. Interconnected computers allowed multiplayer online games. The first were called MUDs, acronym of multiple-user dungeons/ domains. These were text-based games, which hundreds of people could play at once. Players could interact by typing normal(ish) language commands such as "say," "look at *X*," "search room," "kiss *playername*," and "attack *X*."

You could explore, solve puzzles, and form teams, but it was the added social dimension that taught me an important lesson. When you are interacting with other humans, real social behavior with real psychological effects happens. Even though everyone knows it's "just a game," when someone is flirting with you, your palms sweat, you feel attractive, and your heart skips a beat. When someone is trying to kill you, your blood pressure increases, your heart races, your palms sweat, and you feel fear, even though it's just words on a screen and you know you're safe in your house. This is the power of video games – to affect your thoughts, physiology, and feelings. This is, of course, what makes them fun. We get to feel and experience things we wouldn't or couldn't in our "real" lives. Knowing it's a game does not mean it doesn't influence us – in fact, we *want* to be influenced! If we play a game (or watch a movie or show) and it doesn't affect us, we call it "boring."

I became friends with many of the players and still interact with many of them to this day. Many I've never met in person, and yet I know a lot about their daily stresses and habits, their relationships, and we talk and support each other on the game itself. This taught me that the distinction many people make between virtual and real is much more apparent than actual. What I experienced was that any time you get humans together, what happens is real human behavior. People meet, form friendships and enmities, flirt, fall in love, argue, say mean things to each other, fall out of love, and so on. It is similar to what would happen if we locked 100 people in a room for a month, except that it happens at breakneck speed. The life cycle of relationships is incredibly accelerated, partly because in a game there are none of the normal social inhibitors present. As proof of the power of games, I married a woman whom I met on a game.

In 1996, the National Institute on Media and the Family was created. I was working in market research and was hired to conduct national research on what parents wanted in media ratings: the short answer – they want it all (Gentile, Maier, Hasson, & de Bonetti, 2011). Our research resulted in congressional hearings again because the study showed that parents disagree with most of the existing media ratings (Walsh & Gentile, 2001). I became Director of Research, where I was tasked with conducting research to answer the questions that parents, educators, pediatricians, and policy-makers have about media and children's health. The majority of my career has continued to be focused here.

By today, games have become art, by which I mean that they can leave the viewer changed. I continued to be involved in gaming, mostly as a player (all-time favorite: *Beatles Rock Band*), but also in writing code and doing some voice-acting in a game. Although the video game industry tried at times to portray me as being "anti-video game" (Entertainment Software Association, 2011), it should be clear that nothing could be further from the truth. As both a gamer and a scientist (and as a father), I have been aware of how games can have both beneficial and harmful effects.

Why write this Element? My coauthor is my father, SUNY Distinguished Teaching Professor Emeritus of Educational Psychology. Over the years, we recognized that many of the so-called controversies that exist around the video game literature might be at least partially resolved by a deeper understanding of the many categories and phases of learning and how these processes are at the core of many of the effects games can have.

1.1 Why Consider Video Games?

For more than 50 years, social and developmental psychologists have been studying the various ways in which mass media can influence viewers. To oversimplify, social psychologists tend to focus on how the situational contexts can affect people and how these contextual factors may interact with dimensions of people's personalities. Developmental psychologists tend to focus on how people change either with maturation or as a function of particular experiences. In the past 20 years, a great deal of research has focused on video games.

Video games quickly moved from being a niche product to a normative pastime. In 1999, in the United States, the average time children aged between 8 and 18 played video games was 26 minutes a day. By 2004, it was up to 49 minutes. By 2009, it was up to an hour and 13 minutes, with 87 percent of homes having at least one video game console (Rideout, Foehr, & Roberts, 2010). Five years later, the average time playing games among teen gamers had risen to 2 hours and 25 minutes, and by 2019, it was up to almost 3 hours a day (Rideout & Robb, 2019), with time being split between console gaming, computer gaming, and handheld (e.g., mobile phone) gaming. As would be expected, the amount of money spent on video games has also increased dramatically. In the United States alone, sales grew from $5.5 billion in 2000 to about $15 billion in 2019 (Grubb, 2020; Statista Research Department, 2016). Worldwide, about $150 billion was spent on video games in 2019 (Maher, 2019).

As video games became more popular and the amount of time spent began to increase, we received questions such as whether parents should worry about children playing games where they were shooting at other players, or whether it was good that children with attention deficit disorders could play games for hours on end when they couldn't attend to other things for more than 15 minutes. As these questions arose, researchers began to conduct studies to answer them.

Researchers also wondered if the effects of games would be similar to the effects of other media such as television and movies. For example, by the end of the 1990s, it was generally scientifically accepted that watching violent television could increase aggressive thoughts, feelings, and behaviors (e.g., American Academy of Pediatrics, American Psychological Association, American Academy of Child & Adolescent Psychiatry, & American Medical Association, 2000; Comstock & Rubenstein, 1972; Huesmann & Eron, 1986; Pearl, 1982a, 1982b). Would playing violent video games have similar or different effects?

There were many theoretical reasons to expect that the effects might be greater for video games. For example, the television and film literature had shown that identification with aggressive characters increased the likelihood of adopting the aggressive attitudes or behaviors of those characters. In a show, however, it is hard to predict with which character you might identify – you might identify with the victim, in which case your odds of behaving aggressively go down. But in a violent video game, especially in First-Person Shooter (FPS) games, you are required to identify with and take the perspective of the aggressive character. Similarly, games require active participation in aggressive decision-making and behaviors, whereas the viewer is simply a passive observer of violent films or shows. Another reason games were expected to have a larger effect was because the action in violent games tended to be more continuous than it is in film or television. Earlier research had suggested that uninterrupted violence had greater effects on viewers (Donnerstein, Slaby, & Eron, 1994), but most violent films and shows tend to break up the violence because people can become desensitized as they are watching it. Several more theoretical reasons were postulated that tended to predict that violent games would have a larger effect than other violent media (see Gentile & Anderson, 2003 for a list of seven reasons), but the research done over the past 20 years has not tended to show that (more will be said about this later). The effect sizes for violent video games seem to be about the same as for violent TV and movies.

Despite the general consistency with the research on television and film, some scholars claim that there is a "controversy," that there is "no consensus," and that the link between media violence and aggression is an "urban legend" (e.g., Ferguson & Beresin, 2017; Ferguson, Brown, & Torres, 2018). More will be said about this in Section 7.

Our goal with this Element is to describe the wide range of scientific literature on video game effects and to demonstrate how examining the findings from the perspective of the General Learning Model (GLM) may help to resolve some of the apparent controversies.

2 Research on the Psychological Effects of Video Games

Many different psychological aspects of the effects of video games have been studied. This is not the place for a detailed examination of all of them, but we will discuss some of the important aspects and some of the "classic" studies in the areas of violent games, prosocial games, stereotypes, perceptual skills, attention problems, health games, and gaming disorder. As psychologists, we assume that the effects of games are not monolithic but that experience with something can influence emotions, cognitions, and behaviors. There are hundreds of more studies than are reported here, including some that appear contradictory. We encourage interested readers to examine these literatures in more detail than we are able to provide.

2.1 Violent Video Games

Video game violence has been studied more than any other single aspect of gaming. There are now hundreds of published studies, reviews, and meta-analyses (see Plante, Anderson, Allen, Groves, & Gentile, 2020, for a summary). These include

- true experiments, in which we are able to conclude that the violent games *caused* an increase in aggression,
- cross-sectional studies, in which we are able to see how violent game play is associated with real-world aggression, and
- longitudinal studies, in which we follow people across time to see how earlier violent game play is related to later aggression.

All three types of studies tend to find significant effects (Anderson et al., 2010), but what is meant by aggression and violence? Aggression is a behavior intended to cause harm, which would be avoided by the victim if he/she knew about the aggressor's intent (Anderson & Bushman, 2002c; Geen, 2001). It can be any behavior – physical, verbal, or relational. It means that accidents are not aggression as they do not include the intent to harm. The definition of violence, however, is a little fuzzier. It is an extreme subtype of aggression, in that it is physical only, and is extreme such that, if successful, it would result in serious bodily harm or death. Almost all of the studies examine violent game effects on *aggression*, not on *violence*.

The first classic study was published in 2000 (Anderson & Dill, 2000). In their experimental study, 210 late adolescents were randomly assigned to play either a violent or a nonviolent video game. These games had been pretested and shown to be equivalent on many dimensions such as influencing systolic blood pressure, diastolic blood pressure, and heart rate. There were also no differences in the ratings of game difficulty, enjoyment, frustration, or action speed, which is important because frustration can increase aggression (e.g., if the nonviolent game was more difficult, less fun, or more frustrating, we might actually expect the nonviolent gamers to behave more aggressively). Imagine yourself arriving at a laboratory and being told that you are going to play games on the computer, some by yourself and some with a partner. You play a game where you can shoot and kill other characters, and they are trying to shoot you. After playing for 15 minutes, you are given a word completion survey, and then you play another game with another partner. This game is to see who can be fastest, and the experimenter tells you that they are interested in observing how punishment affects performance. You get to set punishment levels for your partner, and they get to set them for you. What you don't know is that it's all programmed and you will win half of the trials. What the experimenters were interested in is how easily aggressive concepts came to your mind and how harshly you punished your partner. If people played the violent game, aggressive thoughts came to their mind more readily, and they were also slightly more aggressive in their behaviors toward another partner.

This study garnered a great deal of attention in the press because it was released shortly after the Columbine High School massacre. This was unfortunate because it set the tone for how the press tended to report on video game studies – violent games either did or did not cause school shootings. Notice that the Anderson & Dill (2000) study says nothing about shootings. Participants gave longer painfully loud noise blasts to an opponent. This is an aggressive behavior but not a violent one. Nonetheless, this changed the way most people think about media violence research, always making it seem extreme when, in fact, the majority of research focuses on everyday levels of aggression – saying unkind things, spreading rumors, threatening, giving people the "cold shoulder," and so on. These are real-life and common aggressive behaviors. When your child comes home crying because someone has been teasing her, it is serious aggression to you. But, no, it's not criminal violence.

As an example, another early study of more than 600 US eighth and ninth graders asked the students which games they played, and how violent they were, and questioned them about their attitudes and behaviors (Gentile, Lynch, Linder, & Walsh, 2004). Children who played more violent video games saw the world more in terms of hostility, received worse grades in school, got into more arguments with teachers (a real-world antisocial behavior), and had been in more physical fights in the past year. If you're a good skeptic, and we want you to be, you might say that perhaps this isn't about violent gaming at all but is instead about being a more naturally aggressive and hostile child. High-hostile children tend to have a more hostile worldview, get poorer grades, get into more arguments, get into more fights, and also play more violent video games – that is accurate.

In this study, however, we measured the children's hostile personality. If we split the children into quartiles on both hostility and violent game exposure, we see that both matter. As seen in Figure 2, the group with the greatest likelihood ·to have been involved in physical fights was the group high on both hostility and violent game play.

Two aspects strike us as interesting. First, the least naturally hostile children who play a lot of violent video games are *more likely* to have been involved in

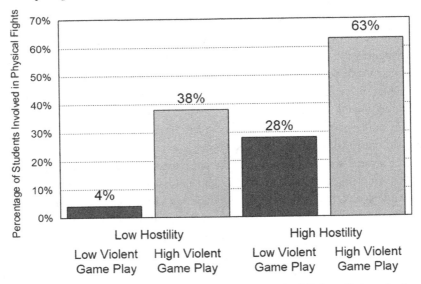

Figure 2 Percentage of students involved in a physical fight split by whether they are high or low on trait hostility and high or low on violent video game exposure (Gentile, Lynch, Linder, & Walsh, 2004)

fights than the most naturally hostile children who do not play violent games (middle two bars). But even more interesting than this is that these data demonstrate the stacking of risk factors. No one thing predicts human aggression – we are more complicated than that. What predicts it well, however, is when someone has several risk factors for aggression and almost no protective factors (Gentile & Bushman, 2012; Gentile & Sesma, 2003; Prot & Gentile, 2014; US Surgeon General, 2001).

This study can tell us something about whether violent gaming is associated with real-world aggression, but it can't tell us much about causality. Nonetheless, experimental studies can tell us about causality, but they usually can't use real-world aggression for ethical reasons. Longitudinal studies can connect the two. By following children across time, we can know what happens first and what second, and we can use measures of real aggression.

There are fewer longitudinal studies than experimental or cross-sectional ones. One followed more than 3,000 children across 2 years, with measurements being made in 3 different years (Gentile, Li, Khoo, Prot, & Anderson, 2014). We found that children who played more violent video games in year 1 had more aggressive cognitions by year 2 and then behaved more aggressively by year 3.

We measured three types of aggressive cognitions in this study. The first was hostile attribution bias. We all know people who, when something annoying happens, can give the other person the benefit of the doubt. We also know people who take everything very personally. Hostile attribution bias is more like that – you have a bias toward attributing hostility to other people's actions. In a violent game, you practice anticipating and expecting others to behave aggressively toward you, and we found that violent gamers increased their hostile attribution biases.

The second type of aggressive cognition we measured was normative beliefs about aggression. This measures how acceptable you believe it is to retaliate when provoked. Again, we all know people who feel you should turn the other cheek. We also know people who feel you should hit back harder. A person with high normative beliefs is more like this – believing it is acceptable to react aggressively when provoked. In a violent game, you get rewarded for behaving aggressively when provoked, and you often get punished if you don't (e.g., you die, lose levels). We found that violent gamers increased their normative beliefs about aggression over time.

The third aggressive cognition we measured was aggressive fantasies. Simply put, this is about how much time people spend thinking about how they would like to behave aggressively toward others, and the entire time you are playing a violent game you are rehearsing an aggressive fantasy. We found that violent gamers increased their aggressive fantasizing.

These three types of aggressive cognitions then predicted increased real-world aggressive behavior (Figure 3). Again, it is not in a simplistic mechanistic way. But it did increase the odds measurably and reliably. We also know that

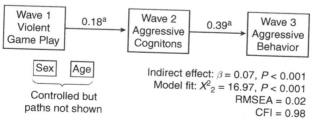

Figure 3 Path analysis showing how Wave 1 violent game play significantly predicts Wave 2 aggressive cognitions, which in turn predicts Wave 3 aggressive behavior (Gentile, Li, Khoo, Prot, & Anderson, 2014). Waves are 1 year apart. The numbers on arrows are standardized regression coefficients; [a]$p < .001$

their later aggressive behavior is not what caused their violent video gaming 2 years previously.

This study helps to demonstrate how the effect happens. Imagine a child who has been spending a lot of time playing violent video games. He is in the school hallway when another student bumps into him hard from behind. Because he has been practicing being hyper-vigilant for potential aggression, he no longer assumes that it was an accident but now is more likely to assume that the other student meant to annoy him. That one tiny change in perception shifts the odds for everything that follows. Another thing that is practiced in gaming is to quickly shift your attention toward an aggressive stimulus, so the child will likely turn to see who bumped him and then he'll call to mind options for what he should do in response. The thing humans tend to do, especially when under stress, is the one that is most accessible to conscious thought (this is known as the availability heuristic; e.g., Rothman & Hardin, 1997; Schwarz et al., 1991). The response that is most available is almost always the one that has been practiced the most. If one has played lots of violent games, one has practiced an aggressive response to an aggressive provocation thousands of times, it is most likely that he will feel that he should say something mean or push back. Nonetheless, just having an aggressive thought is not enough to make someone act on it. But because he has been rewarded for acting aggressively in games, the bar has been lowered, making it seem more acceptable that he should react aggressively. You can see how the odds have shifted that he is more likely to push the other child or say some unkind thing. If he does, the odds that this encounter turns into a physical fight skyrocket.

Here is the interesting thing: When the fight erupts in that school hallway, it looks *nothing* like what our violent gamer was practicing in the video games. Children are not *copying* the aggression they see in the media. Instead, it changes the way you perceive the world and the way you think, and you carry the way you see the world and think with you everywhere. This subtly (but predictably) shifts the odds that you will end up in more aggressive encounters over time.

One of the scariest studies we've ever seen was a true randomized experiment, where 8- to 12-year-old children were asked to bring a friend or relative (Chang & Bushman, 2019). Pairs of friends participated, and they were randomized to play one of the three versions of the game *Minecraft*: (1) a violent version with guns that could be used to kill monsters, (2) a violent version with swords that could be used to kill monsters, or (3) a nonviolent version with no weapons and no monsters. The versions were otherwise identical, with the goal being to find as many emeralds as possible in 20 minutes. One child in each pair played the game while the other watched.

After playing, the children were taken to another room with varied toys and games (e.g., Legos, Uno) and were told they could do whatever they wanted while adults watched via a hidden camera. Hidden in a cabinet in the room, however, were two real 9 mm handguns. The firing pins had been removed, and there was no ammunition, so the children were safe, but each gun was able to count trigger pulls.

The first question was whether the children would find the guns, and if so, would they touch them or would they leave them alone and go and tell an adult like they should? Ninety-one percent of the children found the guns despite them being hidden in a closed cabinet – kids are curious and explore a new environment. Of the 220 children who found the gun, only 6 percent (13) of them didn't touch it and went to tell an adult. In contrast, 85 of the children (39 percent) picked it up and didn't tell an adult.

Once children picked it up, what did they do with it? If the children had played one of the violent video game conditions (either with guns or swords), they spent more than double the amount of time holding the gun compared to the children who played the nonviolent version of the game. The most terrifying result from this study, however, was that if children had played the game with guns, they were far more likely to point the found gun at their friend (or at themselves) and pull the trigger! The mean number of trigger pulls was 3.44 pulls in the gun violence condition, 1.50 pulls in the sword violence condition, and 0.19 pulls in the nonviolent game condition. Remember, these children came in with a best friend or sibling, and finding a real gun, they picked it up, pointed it at their friend, and pulled the trigger. They had no way of knowing if the gun was loaded or not, and if they had just played a violent video game, they were willing to pull the trigger while pointing the gun at themselves or their friends/siblings. In addition, analyses revealed that if children tended to watch more violent TV, movies, and video games at home, they were also more likely to pull the trigger.

There are hundreds of studies showing similar effects, often using different measures of aggression and different mediating and moderating variables (c.f., Anderson et al., 2003; Anderson et al., 2017; Gentile, 2014; Plante, Anderson, Allen, Groves, & Gentile, 2020). This is important because if it is a real effect, it should be able to be found almost no matter how we measure it. If it could only be found using one special method, then it probably isn't a very robust phenomenon. Nonetheless, there are also some studies that show no significant effects, as would be expected in any scientific field. Because this has been something of a "hot" topic, we will return to it again in Section 7.

2.2 Prosocial Games

Although violent games usually garner the most attention, there is a growing body examining the effects of playing games with prosocial content – where characters care about other characters and help them, rather than harm them. It turns out that there can be real benefits, both in the short term and the long term.

One experimental study had college students randomly assigned to play either a prosocial game or a neutral game, after which they were given the beginning of stories and asked to complete them (Greitemeyer & Osswald, 2009). An example story: Imagine you are riding your bicycle down a road. As you are crossing an intersection, a car driver violated your right of way. You are forced to slam on your brakes; otherwise a dangerous accident would have happened. The car driver stops in the middle of the intersection and opens the window. What happens next?

Participants' responses to this (and other stories) can be coded to see what types of thoughts they are having. Those who played a prosocial game reported far fewer aggressive thoughts and actions in response to provoking situations. That is, aggressive ideas didn't come to their minds at the rate that they did for people who hadn't just practiced caring about others in games. Not only that, but in follow-up studies, people who played a prosocial game had faster cognitive access to prosocial words (in contrast to those who played a neutral puzzle game; Greitemeyer & Osswald, 2011) and had more positive feelings and lower-state hostility (in contrast to those who played a neutral or a violent game; Saleem, Anderson, & Gentile, 2012b).

Of course, how we think and feel can influence our behaviors, and several studies have now shown that playing prosocial games can predict more prosocial, helpful, and cooperative behaviors, both in the short term and the long term (Gentile et al., 2009; Greitemeyer, Agthe, Turner, & Gschwendtner, 2012; Greitemeyer & Mügge, 2014; Greitemeyer & Osswald, 2010; Saleem, Anderson, & Gentile, 2012a). This association has been verified in large cross-national studies, including in longitudinal samples (Figure 4; Prot et al., 2014). Several studies also seem to demonstrate that one reason playing prosocial games may lead to an increase in prosocial behavior is because it also leads to an increase in empathy – the ability to notice others' feelings and to see their point of view (Greitemeyer, Osswald, & Brauer, 2010; Prot et al., 2014).

2.3 Stereotypes and Prejudice

No one is born prejudiced against any specific group, although prejudice seems to be fairly easy to acquire. A stereotype is generally defined as a set of shared beliefs about a group. Stereotypes don't necessarily have to be negative.

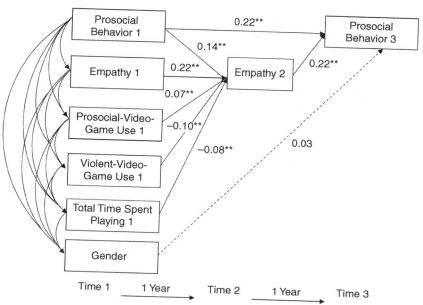

Figure 4 Path analysis showing how Wave 1 prosocial game play significantly predicts Wave 2 empathy, which in turn predicts Wave 3 prosocial behavior, even after controlling for initial levels of prosocial behavior (Prot et al., 2014). Waves are 1 year apart. ** = p < .01

They could include positive ideas (e.g., Italian men are romantic), neutral ones (e.g., university professors are absent-minded), or negative beliefs (e.g., Arabs are terrorists).

The Stereotype Content Model suggests that stereotypes include perceptions on two dimensions: warmth and competence (Fiske, Cuddy, Glick, & Xu, 2002). Groups high in both perceived warmth and competence (usually a group of which one is a member) tend to elicit feelings of admiration and pride, whereas a group low in both (e.g., drug addicts) tends to elicit feelings of anger, disgust, or resentment.

Once a stereotype has been formed, it can easily become prejudice. As Fiske and Taylor (1991, p. 410) note, stereotypes activate a "range of preferences, evaluations, moods, and emotions." Because our actions are dependent on our thoughts and feelings, prejudice can easily become discrimination: behaviors that discriminate against a person or group because of their group membership.

Video games have been studied far less than other media, but the early work seems to confirm that playing games can activate stereotypes and prejudice. Content analyses of video game play, video game ads, and video game covers certainly suggest stereotyped representations exist in video games (Burgess, Dill, Stermer, Burgess, & Brown, 2011; Dill, Gentile, Richter, & Dill, 2005). In general, female characters are underrepresented, are more often secondary characters, and are hypersexualized when shown (Downs & Smith, 2010; Lynch, Tompkins, van Driel, & Fritz, 2016). Similarly, minority characters are underrepresented and are stereotypically represented, such that Blacks are highly likely to be portrayed as athletes or criminals and Asians are highly likely to be portrayed as martial artists (Behm-Morawitz & Ta, 2014).

Because the portrayals are stereotyped, it is certainly possible that spending more time playing games could cultivate stereotyped views, and this is exactly what has been found. A survey of White undergraduates found that those who spent more time playing video games also had less egalitarian views of Blacks (Behm-Morawitz & Ta, 2014). Similarly, a large representative survey of more than 13,000 French adolescents found that youth who spent more time playing video games also held more sexist views of women, after controlling for age, sex, socioeconomic level, religiosity, and television viewing (Bègue, Sarda, Gentile, Bry, & Roché, 2017).

Randomized experiments have also provided evidence that video games can cultivate negative stereotypes. In one experiment, White participants who played as a Black avatar had more accessible hostile thoughts (Eastin, Appiah, & Cicchirllo, 2009). In another, players were exposed to both violent and nonviolent games each with both White and Black characters (Burgess, Dill, Stermer, Burgess, & Brown, 2011). Participants were faster at linking violent stimuli following games with Black characters and at linking nonviolent stimuli with White characters. These studies demonstrate that images of video game characters can evoke and strengthen racial stereotypes.

We do not mean to suggest that there is no room for nuance. The effects of video games (or any other media) are not monolithic, and they do not necessarily affect everyone identically. For example, in one experimental study examining in-game behavior when playing with a White or Black avatar, players playing with a Black avatar were more aggressive, particularly if they were high on embodied identification – that is, if they "lost themselves" more in the character (Ash, 2016). Those who didn't experience a sense of embodied merging with the character did not show the effect.

One remarkable pair of experimental studies found that games could not only prime stereotypes but also apparently shift prejudicial attitudes (Saleem & Anderson, 2013). In the first, 224 participants were randomly assigned to play either a nonviolent game with no specific ethnicities present, a violent game where the opponents are Russian terrorists, or the same violent game with Arab terrorists. People who played the violent game with Arab terrorists endorsed more anti-Arab prejudicial attitudes. This study included a clever way to measure stereotypes. Everyone was asked to draw the "typical" Caucasian man and woman and Arab man and woman. Those who had played the game against Arab terrorists drew both Arab men and women more stereotypically and also tended to draw Arab men with a weapon and negative expression. In contrast, they drew Caucasian men and women as generally happy and professional (Figure 5). The surprise in this study was that playing against Russian terrorists *also* increased negative attitudes about Arabs, despite there being no Arab cues in that game. This is likely due to the high saturation of news stories pairing words such as "Arab" and "Muslim" with "terrorist."

A second study included two more games – a nonviolent game with an Arab character and a violent game with no terrorism theme. They also included a measure of feelings about different ethnic groups (Black, Latino, Arab). Playing the terrorism-themed video game produced significantly greater anti-Arab attitudes and more negative feelings toward Arabs compared to those who played nonviolent games or even a violent game without elements of terrorism. The authors noted that the combined results "imply that in our participant population the terrorism-Arab association is so strong that a reference to terrorism is sufficient to prime a negative Arab attitude even in the absence of a direct Arab reference. It also suggests that violent content, by itself, appears insufficient to prime anti-Arab attitude or affect" (p. 95). The authors also found that people who relied more on media had greater anti-Arab attitudes.

Similar experimental results have been found for sexist attitudes. For example, playing a game with a sexualized female avatar caused greater

Arab Female   Arab Male   Caucasian Female   Caucasian Male

Figure 5 Example drawings of "typical" Arab and Caucasian men and women (from Saleem & Anderson, 2013)

objectification of women and greater acceptance of the rape myth (incorrect attitudes that serve to justify male sexual aggression against women, such as that women secretly want to get raped; Fox, Ralston, Cooper, & Jones, 2015). Another experiment found that playing a game with sexually objectified women primed thoughts related to sex, increased viewing of women as sex objects, and predicted higher likelihood of sexual harassment (Yao, Mahood, & Linz, 2010).

Games do not have to possess these effects, however. Games could be designed intentionally to undermine stereotypes and prejudice. One clever study focused on an effect called stereotype threat. Essentially, when you are a member of a stereotyped group, you may act in a more stereotypical manner once the stereotype is made salient. For example, women perform more poorly at math tasks if the stereotype that men are better at math is primed (Spencer, Steele, & Quinn, 1999). Ratan and Sah (2015) had women complete a competitive math task after playing a sword-fighting game. Those who used a male avatar performed better on the math task than those playing with a female avatar, particularly if they had spent time customizing how it looks and felt less embodied in their avatars. The authors noted how self-relevance, customization, and embodiment of avatars could reduce stereotype threat, thereby showing that digital games can be designed to maximize positive outcomes. Nonetheless, because games overall tend to support negative stereotypes about women and minorities, higher exposure to video games is likely to create or increase stereotypes and prejudice.

2.4 Perceptual Skills

Some of the most well-documented benefits of video games, including fast-paced violent games, include improvements in perceptual skills. Researchers Green and Bavelier recognized that many first-person shooter games have regular features, including (a) fast pace, (b) the necessity to scan the full screen regularly and to react and focus attention quickly on particular areas, (c) the value of maintaining awareness of the environment behind, above, and below you, (d) the ability to track multiple moving objects at once and (e) the ability to detect small changes in color or shape. They labeled these types of games "action" games and hypothesized that spending time on them could cause changes to perceptual abilities.

An early set of five studies demonstrated that action game players (compared to nongamers or gamers who don't play these types of games) had greater attentional capacity to maintain awareness of multiple objects, could keep count of a greater number of independent objects, had a wider useful field of view (that is, they could see farther out into their periphery), and could gather information off of a screen much faster (Green & Bavelier, 2003). Four of the studies were correlational, so a critic might argue that different types of people play different types of games. Their fifth study, however, randomly assigned people to play one of two games for an hour a day for 10 consecutive days. One was an action game and the other was *Tetris*, which also includes a challenging visuospatial motor component but rewards focusing on one object at a time rather than distributing attention around the screen. Both groups improved at all three types of tasks – enumerating multiple objects, useful field of view, and speed of processing – but the group playing the action game improved much more.

This research team replicated and extended these studies, often taking non-gamers and having them play 30 or 50 hours of an action game or other games. Action games can influence many visual perceptual skills, including improving spatial resolution both centrally and in the periphery (Green & Bavelier, 2007), increasing speed and accuracy of responding to visual cues (Dye, Green, & Bavelier, 2009), enhancing simultaneous multiple object tracking (Green & Bavelier, 2006), and improving the ability to detect small changes in shading or color (Li, Polat, Makous, & Bavelier, 2009). There is also some evidence that the gender gap in spatial abilities can be reduced or eliminated with video games (Ratan, Shen, & Williams, 2020; Subrahmanyam & Greenfield, 1994).

If this all seems a bit esoteric, consider the skills an air traffic controller needs. She is staring at a radar screen, and she needs to be able to track multiple objects at once, detect tiny changes as they occur, even if they occur at the edge of the screen, shift visual attention rapidly, and gather information quickly and accurately. All of these skills can be improved by playing action video games, although there are some criticisms of how far any of these skills may transfer (Boot, Blakely, & Simons, 2011).

2.5 Attention Deficit Problems

Perhaps ironically, given all of the benefits to visual attention skills just mentioned, there is also a small body of research demonstrating game use increasing attention deficit problems. A cross-sectional sample of college students found that both the amount of time spent watching television and the amount spent playing video games correlated positively with attention problems as measured by adult Attention Deficit Hyperactivity Disorder (ADHD) and impulsiveness scales (Swing, Gentile, Anderson, & Walsh, 2010). It is, of course, unclear from this study whether the screen time is causing attentional difficulties or if people with lower ability to focus and maintain attention are drawn to fast-paced screen media. A longitudinal study of more than 1,300 third- to fifth-grade students, however, similarly found that children's TV and video game time predicted increased attention problems a year later, as rated by classroom teachers (Swing, Gentile, Anderson, & Walsh, 2010).

This finding was somewhat startling for at least two reasons. First, much of the work on attention deficit problems over the past 40 years has focused on the genetic and biological aspects of attentional control. This has led to the development of several useful medications, but it has also kept much of the focus on biological risk factors. Almost all human psychological issues have both "nature" and "nurture" aspects, and we are just beginning to explore the nurture side. The second surprise was that attention problems could change measurably in just 1 year, predicted by how much time children were spending on electronic screens.

A later study followed more than 3,000 children across 3 years, finding evidence of bidirectionality (Gentile, Swing, Lim, & Khoo, 2012). That is, difficulty maintaining attention or impulsiveness predicted more time spent playing video games. Simultaneously, spending more time playing video games also predicted more attention problems and impulsivity.

A study of college students found some intriguing evidence for the neural basis of these findings (Bailey, West, & Anderson, 2010). Both high and low gamers were recruited and were connected to an electroencephalogram (EEG) machine, which reads the spatial and temporal functioning of the brain in response to stimuli. The students completed a task, which measured both proactive and reactive control.[1] Proactive control represents a future-oriented form of regulation that primes the information-processing system before the onset of a critical stimulus. That is, you get ready to react quickly because you are expecting something to happen. Reactive control, in contrast, is a form of regulation implemented when conflict or ambiguity arises. That is, when you are surprised by something, can you react quickly to it?

We might expect that experienced gamers would be better at both types of attentional control, as many games reward both planning and reacting. We would be wrong. There was little difference between the high and low gamers on reactive control, but there were significant differences in proactive control. High gamers were unable to maintain proactive control, which is necessary for maintaining attention. This is important not only because attentional control is

---

[1] The type of task is called a Stroop task. Although there are several versions, the best known is trying to say the names of colors of words, but the words are color names. Thus, you might see the word "red" in green ink, and you have to say "green." By measuring the differences in speed between when the words and ink colors are consistent or inconsistent, you can see how difficult it is to inhibit an impulse (reactive control) as well as how much consistency helps (proactive control).

important for school success, but also because lower attentional control is a risk factor for aggressive behavior (Barlett, Gentile, Barlett, Eisenmann, & Walsh, 2012; Swing & Anderson, 2014).

Although there is only a small body of research on this topic, it is supported by the growing literature on the effects of media multitasking. The classic study (Ophir, Nass, & Wagner, 2009) showed that people who think they are good at multitasking are actually worse at it in reality and also that people who spend more time multitasking are *worse* at it than people who don't! We usually get better at things we practice, so why is it that more multitasking doesn't make us better at multitasking? The likely reason is that what one is really practicing is being easily distracted.

There is sometimes a perceived conflict between the research on improved visual attentional skills and that on attention deficit problems. We see no conflict, other than that these two camps mean something very different when they use the term "attention." The perceptual skills that are gained from games include ability to notice small changes in the periphery and quickly shift the focus of attention. This is very different from what classroom teachers mean by attention, where they want you to not be distracted by the child fidgeting at the desk next to you. This takes proactive control and the ability to tune out irrelevant distractions, whereas games appear better at training dividing attention.

2.6 Health Games

It should be little surprise, given the research already reviewed, that many of the effects games can have could be used intentionally for medical rehabilitation. For example, the improvements in visual processing as a result of playing action games could be beneficial for treating issues such as amblyopia and dyslexia. Amblyopia (colloquially called "lazy eye") is a common issue where information is favored from one eye, making the other perceptually weaker. Despite being resistant to treatment after childhood, adults who played games for about 80 hours improved their vision substantially more than adults given the standard eye-patching rehabilitation procedure (Li, Ngo, Nguyen, & Levi, 2011). The authors noted that the "recovery in visual acuity that we observed is at least 5-fold faster than would be expected from occlusion therapy in childhood amblyopia" (p. 1). Similarly, playing action games for 80 minutes for only 9 days improved dyslexic children's reading speed, "without any cost in accuracy, more so than 1 year of spontaneous reading development and more than or equal to highly demanding traditional reading treatments" (Franceschini et al., 2013, p. 462).

These results take advantage of the existing structural and mechanical dimensions of games (Gentile, 2011), but one could also design games for particular goals. Indeed, there is a growing field specifically examining "serious games" (e.g., https://seriousgamessociety.org/) where games are designed to produce multiple societal benefits such as energy conservation, improving corporate teamwork, and enhancing classroom instruction.

This is not new, as any computerized simulation trainer would count, such as training pilots with flight simulator software (Gopher, Weil, & Bareket, 1994). What is new, perhaps, is the wide array of important issues that inventive people have tackled with games. We cannot review them all here, but some of the early classic studies showed that if children with serious chronic health issues such as asthma or diabetes played video games designed to help them recognize their symptoms and know how and when to respond (e.g., with medicine), these children were more compliant with their health-care behaviors than if children read exactly the same information in a pamphlet (e.g., Lieberman, 1997, 2001a, 2001b). Similarly, general popular games and specifically designed games have been used to help elderly patients recover balance, strength, and even maintain greater mental health (e.g., Pope, Zeng, & Gao, 2017; Xu, Liang, Baghaei, Wu Berberich, & Yue, 2020). Gaming may even be beneficial for surgeons (Rosser, Gentile, Hanigan, & Danner, 2012; Rosser et al., 2007).

2.7 Gaming Disorder

I (Doug) first began studying what people colloquially call video game "addiction" back in 1999 because even then parents were talking about their children being addicted to games, and I did not believe them. I believed that parents simply meant, "My child spends a lot of time on games and I don't understand why." This isn't the same as an addiction. Addictions are not defined as doing something a lot – they are defined as *dysfunction*. That is, for something to rise to the level that it would be a clinical disorder, it must be damaging multiple areas of one's life. I believed that there was no way games were doing that and began conducting studies to show that games were not dysfunctional for anyone. I was wrong. The more I studied it from this clinical perspective, the more I couldn't disprove it.

Harris Polls helped me collect national data from more than a thousand 8- to 18-year-olds. We found that most children play video games but that 8.5 percent of those gamers could be considered to have a serious problem (Gentile, 2009). Many more studies followed, and by 2013, the American Psychiatric Association added internet gaming disorder to the appendix of the Diagnostic and Statistical Manual, version 5 (DSM5). This signaled that the early research appeared strong but that more studies were needed. By 2019, the research had become clear enough that the World Health Organization included gaming disorder in the International Classification of Diseases, version 11 (ICD-11; World Health Organization, 2019). Although exact prevalence rates vary greatly based on sample characteristics and screening tools, the percentage appears to be between 1 percent and 10 percent of gamers (Fam, 2018; Mihara & Higuchi, 2017). On the one hand, this is good news because it means that more than 90 percent can play games without causing serious damage to their lives. On the other hand, however, this is a large number of people, given that most children and a growing percentage of adults are regular video game players.

At this point, much is known about gaming disorder (Gentile et al., 2017), although many issues still remain to be resolved. There are several different methods for screening for it, but they tend to lead to similar conclusions. It seems likely to be comorbid with several other mental health issues; it is probably not simply a symptom of other disorders but independently adds to the risk (Rokkum & Gentile, 2018). Once someone has begun having trouble with gaming, it predicts poorer adjustment up to 6 years later (Coyne et al., 2020). The deficits include both personal aspects (e.g., depression, anxiety) and social aspects such as aggression and social isolation (e.g., Coyne et al., 2020; Gentile, 2009; Gentile et al., 2011; Griffiths, 2000; Liu et al., 2018; Wartberg, Kriston, Zieglmeier, Lincoln, & Kammerl, 2019; Yee, 2001).

2.8 Summary

This section covered a great deal of research on the multiple effects video games can have on players, some of which could be intentional effects (e.g., games designed to train health compliance behaviors), and most of which are unintentional (e.g., violent games, stereotypes, gaming disorder). There are still more scientifically documented effects that are not covered here, and these myriad effects do not appear to be all that similar to each other. What ties them all together? Learning.

At their core, most media effects are based on learning and practice. Although it is certainly true that practice can make perfect,[2] this does not explain the mechanisms through which learning happens. The rest of this Element will focus on the multiple human learning mechanisms that underlie most media effects, and indeed, much of social psychology.

---

[2] This isn't entirely accurate. Modern neuroscience has clarified that practice makes permanent – it builds automaticity and habit. But if you practice something poorly, you get really good at doing it poorly. Only perfect practice makes perfect.

3 Domain-Specific Learning Theories

Social psychologists have done an excellent job examining the mechanisms through which social attitudes and behaviors can be influenced by the environment. Implicit in this approach, however, is that learning underlies these social behaviors. With the exception of Social Learning Theory, however, very few learning models have explicitly described how learning is at the root of many attitudes and behaviors. Furthermore, most learning theories have been discussed in domain-specific terms. We believe that an integrated model can lead to some new insights and testable hypotheses that are not seen when each learning mechanism is considered separately. The GLM (Buckley & Anderson, 2006; Gentile, Groves, & Gentile, 2014; Maier & Gentile, 2012) incorporates each of the domain-specific theories into a metatheoretical model. The GLM may help to generate new hypotheses by developing links between the levels of analysis described by each domain-specific theory. This volume provides the full model as it stands today. First, however, we briefly describe several of the specific learning mechanisms, thereafter we describe how they may be integrated into the general model.

3.1 Brain Functions and Developmental Foundations of Learning and Memory

From birth, infants are embedded in a rich array of social and physical environments interacting with their proliferating number of synapses. This proliferating stage of brain development, called *synaptogenesis*, forms synapses far in excess of eventual adult levels (Bruer, 1997). At the same time, individual synapses become more receptive to stimuli that are repeated – a process called *potentiation*. After some months of synaptogenesis, synaptic pruning begins and continues for years, resulting in fewer synapses as adults than in infancy.

Which synapses are preserved? Those that were repeatedly stimulated, most commonly but not necessarily, by purposeful practice. As Hebb's axiom (1949) states, *the neurons that fire together, wire together.*

Our nervous systems are, of course, neither monolithic in structure nor linear in function. Sensory receptors are connected to various parts of the brain, each of which has specific functions, such as maintaining body operations (brain stem), generating emotions and consolidating memories (limbic system), enabling speech and other cognitive acts (cerebrum), and coordinating movement (cerebellum). But each of these is connected to and continually interactive with the other systems. Moreover, when one brain system or location is incapacitated, others may take over its functions. Thus, in contrast to the popular ideas of right versus left brain typologies, the brain operates much more holistically – with simultaneous parallel and multivariate processing of stimuli in many parts of the brain.

Perhaps the earliest comprehensive explanation was attempted by Hebb (1959), who suggested that repeatedly stimulated synapses would produce *cell assemblies*, the brain's base for the automatized, relatively effortless performances of content or skills that have been mastered. Current research uses brain scan technologies Hebb could not have imagined, but they roughly support his conceptions (Langille & Brown, 2018).

Each of the specific processes, types, or domains of learning to be considered in the following sections likely has primary brain sites activated and involved, but all interact with secondary or tertiary sites (e.g., attitudes have both conceptual and emotional components). Therefore, even as we describe specific domains or types of learning, we also need to consider the interactions among them.

3.2 Sensation, Perception, and Habituation

If *sensation* is defined as stimulation of one or more of our senses (e.g., auditory, visual, tactile), then it is a neurological act that is precursor to but probably not yet recognizable as a cognitive act. *Perception*, in contrast, is usually defined as an active cognitive process of making sense of sensations, that is, attributing meaning to them (e.g., Neisser, 1967). Perception therefore benefits from prior knowledge or experience to achieve the "analysis by synthesis" capabilities, which Neisser posited as central to any theory of cognition.

When a stimulus is first presented, it elicits an orienting response and *attention* to that stimulus. Repeat that stimulus, however, and there will be a decrease in the time spent attending to it. *Habituation* has occurred, which implies familiarity with the stimulus – an elementary but important type of learning. Repeatedly show a baby a picture of a person and measure the amount of time the baby looks at it. After as few as three presentations, the baby's time attending to the picture will begin to decrease. This is taken as evidence of learning: The baby can recognize that picture. All that is needed for habituation learning is exposure to a stimulus. In fact, even a single exposure that is too fast to be consciously noticed can change behavior (Bridger, 1961; Colombo & Mitchell, 2009).

Habituation also accounts for our ability to learn to tolerate noxious or threatening situations. When you first enter a noisy space, the noise is jarring. Remain there for a while, however, and you will get accustomed to that level of noise, while a newcomer will wonder how you can tolerate that noise. This also implies that the noise level can be gradually increased over time and you will become habituated to it and learn to tolerate that which was previously intolerable.

For example, in an experiment where one group of men repeatedly viewed sexually violent films, experimental participants expressed significantly less sympathy for domestic violence victims, and rated their injuries as less severe, than did a no-exposure comparison group (Mullin & Linz, 1995). Tolerance to spousal abuse, noxious smells, and media violence can all be at least partly explained by habituation (see Sidman, 1960, for other examples).

3.3 Perception and Attention

If a white ivory ball is sitting on a table, its attributes will hardly be noticed. Now, in full view of an observer, replace that ball with a red one. Immediately an attribute of both balls – their color – will become salient. Let an egg replace the red ball, and the shape will come into focus. Replace the egg with a tennis ball, and the hardness emerges as an attribute. And thus (as this example from Martineau in James, 1890, demonstrates) what was first merely an object becomes, in turn, a white, spherical, and hard object. Contrasts, in other words, focus our attention toward salient details or dimensions that help us understand the meaning of what we see.

Context and prior knowledge are also determinants of what we perceive. One study asked people to test the quality of headphones by listening to sentences. Four of the sentences had a phoneme missing at the beginning of a word, so what was always heard was the sound "eel." They heard (1) the *eel was on the axle, (2) the *eel was on the shoe, (3) the *eel was on the orange, and (4) the *eel was on the table. When asked what was heard, no one said "eel." Instead, they reported hearing the *wheel* was on the axle, the *heel* was on the shoe, the *peel* was on the orange, and the *meal* was on the table (Warren & Warren, 1970).

If we are actively attempting to make sense of sensations, as these examples imply, then we must be interpreting whatever we encounter in terms of what we already know. This principle of top-down processing – that new information can be rendered meaningful by reference to what we already know – provides the base upon which new learning occurs (as well as its rate of acquisition). For example, video games often provide training periods to help players learn what to pay attention to on the screen and to know what various symbols "mean." This learning allows for learning of more complicated situations or combinations in the future.

3.4 Discrimination

Humans use not only top-down processing, as described earlier, but also bottom-up processing. We can learn to distinguish two or more things that are not the same, a type of learning sometimes called discrimination (or perceptual learning, which is a bit broader; Gibson, 1963, 1969; Gibson & Pick, 2000).[3] Discrimination learning only requires repeated exposures for learning to occur. It usually helps if the repeated exposures provide an opportunity for comparison. For example, if you do not drink wine, and we place five glasses in front of you, telling you that this one is a merlot, this is a cabernet, etc. . . . does not help. They all taste the same to you. Only after you have tried them sufficiently can you begin to notice the differences, and only after you can detect the differences can you begin to associate a name with it.

Discrimination learning relies on detecting differences that already exist in the world. It does not need reinforcement, although reinforcement can speed up perceptual learning. Perceptual learning is therefore dependent on information in the environment that is needed to detect, differentiate, and categorize. This can happen even in manufactured environments such as video games, where repeated play gives players the opportunity to learn to detect affordances and patterns, and notice finer and finer details, which also allows for greater skill and success in playing the games (Green, Li, & Bavelier, 2010).

These types of learning often need to occur prior to other types, such as associative learning. Only after you can discriminate something as being different from other things can you learn to associate it with other things and consequences. That is, habituation and discrimination learning may be necessary conditions for several other learning mechanisms, such as associative, cognitive/semantic, and procedural learning.

3.5 Classical (Respondent) Conditioning

When a biological reflex becomes associated with a previous neutral stimulus, that stimulus can come to elicit a similar reflexive response. Ringing a bell (the conditioned stimulus, or CS) followed by giving food (the unconditioned stimulus, US) trained dogs to salivate to the tone alone (conditioned response, or CR). Salivation (the unconditioned response, UR), as a natural reflex to food in the mouth, did not need to be learned (Pavlov, 1927). A more mnemonic term is *respondent conditioning* (after Skinner, 1938), because it emphasizes that behavior occurs *in response* or reaction to an eliciting stimulus in an involuntary manner.

Pavlov's contemporary, Watson (1913, 1919) was also studying the conditionability of reflexes, as well as trying to catalogue which habits or reflexes

---

[3] In recent years, some attention has been given to how people can extract patterns in language and visual domains, calling it statistical learning (e.g., Aslin & Newport, 2012). It appears to us to be largely a different name for the same mechanisms underlying perceptual learning.

could be considered "natural" and which "learned." As part of that research program, he provided the classic demonstration of conditioned fear in Little Albert by introducing a previously neutral white rat into a room and followed by a loud noise. The noise (US) elicited fear and crying (UR) in the presence of the rat, which on later trials became a CS.

Decades of research demonstrated that much of our emotional responding can be explained by respondent conditioning (e.g., feeling tense at the dentist's clinic; Bower & Hilgard, 1981). Being bullied at school can make one hate school. Despite the apparent ease with which respondent conditioning can occur, there are limits. Generalization to other stimuli goes only so far (Bregman, 1934; Garcia & Ervin, 1968). Nonetheless, conditioned emotions are an important level of learning, which also interact with behavioral and cognitive learning.

3.6 Operant (Instrumental) Conditioning

Whereas respondent conditioning concerns *involuntary* behavior elicited by an unconditioned stimulus, operant or instrumental conditioning is concerned with voluntary or purposeful behavior. This is behavior that is emitted by an organism exploring its environment, often to achieve some desired consequence or goal (Skinner, 1938). Achieving a desired consequence increases the probability of that behavior occurring in the future because the behavior is instrumental in achieving the goal (Thorndike, 1911). The organism learns to control its environment while simultaneously being shaped by the environmental consequences (Skinner, 1974). When this occurs, we say that the behavior has been reinforced (increased in probability in similar situations).

Reinforcement can occur in two ways. *Positive reinforcement* occurs by achieving a positive outcome or desired goal, as when whining achieves a parent's attention, or finishing homework earns a chance to play video games. *Negative reinforcement* occurs by escaping or removing some negative outcome or noxious stimulus, as when a student studies hard (or maybe cheats) to escape a failing grade.

Two other ways in which voluntary behavior is shaped are via extinction and punishment. Extinction is the process of continuous nonreinforcement, which teaches the learner that responding in previously rewarded ways is no longer effective. Thus, the behavior eventually decreases in frequency, though not smoothly because nonreinforcement is frustrating and the behavior has not been forgotten.

Punishment, in contrast, provides an aversive consequence to the behavior (a slap or reprimand: *positive punishment*; or a loss of privileges or a fine:

negative punishment), with the usual effect of suppressing the behavior, at least momentarily in the presence of the punisher.

There are many complexities that accompany extinction and punishment, including frustration effects (e.g., Amsel, 1962) and learned helplessness (e.g., Seligman, 1974, 1975), but these are beyond the scope of this Element (see Hulse, Egeth, & Deese, 1980 for more comprehensive discussion).

Operant conditioning is analogous to Darwin's natural selection: behaviors survive and are maintained because the consequences select them. The consequences therefore are primary in accounting for behaviors and their frequencies. Nevertheless, behaviors occur in a situation or context that provides cues (*discriminative stimuli*) for appropriate behavior, including social behaviors with social consequences. In behavior modification's A-B-Cs, these are the Antecedents, in the presence of which Behaviors occur, and then the Consequences select. Red and green traffic lights cue our stop and go behaviors, but they do not *make* us stop (as in respondent conditioning). Rather, we learn to discriminate when it is appropriate to stop or go, presumably because of the consequences associated with those behaviors (or their converse). Once learned, the cue signals the appropriate behavior and it can become habitual, requiring little conscious control and therefore allowing multitasking.

As one might expect, the more reinforcement a behavior receives, the faster or better the learning at first. But each new reinforcement follows the law of diminishing returns (see Section 5). Even more important than number or amount of reinforcements is therefore the schedule of reinforcement. Intermittent and variable reinforcement produce more consistent behaviors, especially in the face of frustration than continuous or entirely predictable reinforcement (Ferster & Skinner, 1957).

When a behavior is constantly reinforced, the learner comes to expect and rely on that reinforcement. When reinforcement is withdrawn (e.g., the vending machine swallows your coin but does not deliver your purchase), you are frustrated. You may try once more, but will you continue to gamble with the vending machine beyond that? When a behavior has been intermittently and variably reinforced, on the other hand, we learn to tolerate frustration and to persist (resist extinction) despite nonreinforcement – witness gamblers at slot machines (they continue despite losing repeatedly). As we will note later, game creators make use of these principles very effectively.

3.7 Observational (Social) Learning

Research on latent learning demonstrated that learning could occur in the absence of consequences (Tolman, 1932, 1959). By simply observing where food could be obtained, for example, organisms were later able to use this information to negotiate a maze much faster than those who were not able to observe it. Reinforcement is sufficient, but not necessary, for learning.

We can learn simply from seeing others speak and act. For example, kindergarten children were exposed to a model who performed novel aggressive acts (e.g., kicking it, sitting on it, and punching it) and commented (e.g., "Pow, right in the nose!") against an inflated Bobo clown doll. These actions were performed in one of three conditions: a real-life condition by an adult in the room with the child, a filmed version of the same adult but shown on TV, or a cartoon character on TV. After a frustration period, the children were allowed to play with any of the available toys, including the Bobo doll, while being observed and scored for aggressive behaviors and comments. Children in a control group did not witness any modeled aggression. Over all conditions (including male vs. female models), the experimental treatments produced approximately equal amounts of aggression in the child observers, and about twice as much as induced by the control treatment, demonstrating that children learned simply from watching (Bandura, Ross, & Ross, 1963).

In follow-up studies, models were praised or reprimanded for aggressive behaviors (e.g., Bandura, 1965; Bandura & Kupers, 1964). Children did not spontaneously imitate the punished acts, whereas they did imitate the rewarded acts. The punished behaviors had been learned, however, because children were able to demonstrate them later when asked. Thus, as noted earlier, reinforcing or punishing consequences primarily affects performance, not learning. The distinction between learning and performance is important, because we often don't realize we've learned anything until a later experience reminds us of it in some way. This "reminding" does not need to be conscious to influence our feelings and behaviors.

3.8 Cognitive Learning

Human symbolic communication allows for learning without overt action. Thus, humans can learn by associating cognitive concepts together, by creating new mental representations of concepts, and by creating cognitive maps of spatial arrangements. To be able to learn, remember, apply (transfer) knowledge, evaluate, or think about *content* – including to think about or evaluate emotions, behavior, or one's own thinking processes (metacognition) – are cognitive processes. These can occur independent of, in parallel with, or in spite of operant (behavioral) or respondent (emotional) processes. For example, we can work on a math problem to understand it, or we can work on it to finish quickly and escape (negative reinforcement) the anxiety that is often associated with math (respondent conditioning). In either case, the cognitive parts of those experiences operate by different principles than respondent or operant conditioning. Memory, for example, is improved by distributed practice, imagery, and organization of the material. Transfer is facilitated by learning the prerequisites to a high level, understanding the principles on which the required performance is based, and practicing with different strategies under a variety of conditions. These are the topics that we examine in more detail later.

Declarative conceptual information is often described as being linked in associative neural networks of related concepts. Thus, the concept of bird is probably closely related to the concept of sparrow, but less closely related to ostrich, and even less to dinosaur. As we learn that birds are the modern descendants of dinosaurs, we can reorganize our associations between different concepts. Although neural networks are sometimes assumed to be semantic in nature, concepts can also be linked with feelings related to those concepts.

Note that we did not adopt the common classification of *association learning* for operant and respondent processes. This is because a number of cognitive processes are also associative in nature: paired-associates for vocabulary learning or states-capitals, serial position effects in list learning, and imagery techniques as recollection strategies, to name just three.

3.9 Emotional Learning

Emotional learning and memory are related to cognitive learning and memory, albeit a distinct form (Eichenbaum, 2008). The brain has networks, such as in the amygdala, designed specifically to attend to the emotional aspects of situations. These brain circuits support our feelings and expressions of emotions, as well as our learning about the emotional aspects of experiences; they also can change what is learned. There are three major outputs of the amygdala. In response to seeing something (e.g., violent image), one neural response pathway travels to the cerebral cortex to support our conscious awareness of our feelings. A second pathway travels to other memory systems (e.g., in the striatum and hippocampus), which can influence attention and therefore what is learned. A third pathway controls our bodily responses, such as hormone release and the autonomic nervous system (e.g., the "fight or flight" response). One important implication is that emotion plays an important role in attention and motivation to attend (vigilance). Specifically, it moderates attention and memories, and facilitates remembering emotional aspects of experiences and concepts.

When we experience an emotional response (especially when the stress hormones cortisol and epinephrine are released), memory is enhanced. For example, memory performance was significantly related to the amount of amygdala activation for emotionally arousing film clips compared to neutral film clips (Cahill et al., 1996).

Emotional learning underlies many psychological constructs, such as attitudes and biases, which have an emotional component as a core aspect. For example, after the September 11, 2001, attacks in the United States, the media focused on how the attackers were Muslim. Because this fact was associated with such an emotionally negative event, it generalized to negative stereotypes about Muslim people and Arab people (they are not the same people) and to anti-Muslim attitudes (Ahmad, 2006; Saleem, Prot, Anderson, & Lemieux, 2017; Selod, 2015). Emotional learning also usually underlies what is sometimes called "flashbulb memory," vivid, strong, detailed, and long-lasting memories (Brown & Kulik, 1977). It is valuable to remember that emotional learning can also be positive.

3.10 Summary of Individual Mechanisms

Humans have many different ways that they can learn. Some mechanisms are able to demonstrate learning from a single experience, whereas others require repeated experiences, some may happen serially or in parallel, some may support or interfere with others. The vast majority of research has examined each mechanism individually or in contrast to others, but this isn't actually how we learn. Our brains do not only use one at a time. The GLM, described next, attempts to put all of the pieces together into a holistic meta-model.

We intend for the GLM to be broadly applicable to social psychological topics, but for the immediate purposes, we are interested in how it may help to answer some of the questions about the video game effects literature, such as how attitudes may be learned in games and transferred to "real-world" situations.

4 The General Learning Model

The GLM has value as a metatheory because it defines the multiple levels at which learning can occur and how they can work independently or influence each other, rather than focusing only on one or two mechanisms or processes. The GLM incorporates the multiple domain-specific theories and allows for a more complex description of the parallel learning processes at work.

A word is needed about its development. Beginning the 1990s, Craig Anderson and his colleagues recognized that aggression theories tended to be domain-specific. Anderson recognized that they could be combined into a metatheoretical model (Anderson, Deuser, & DeNeve, 1995). This model developed over several years, and was applied to violent video game studies. The full model was described and renamed as the General Aggression Model (Anderson & Bushman, 2002b). Recognizing that learning was the basis for a great deal of what happens underneath the General Aggression Model, Anderson and Buckley suggested that a broader GLM was possible. The first attempt to flesh out that model and apply it to data was in 2009, where we used it to predict the effects of prosocial video games on prosocial behavior (Gentile et al., 2009). The model has been further refined and developed over several more papers (Anderson, Gentile, & Dill, 2012; Gentile, Groves, & Gentile, 2014; Maier & Gentile, 2012) and studies (Saleem, Anderson, & Gentile, 2012a; Saleem, Barlett, Anderson, & Hawkins, 2017). Several other researchers have used the GLM to help guide their research studies (e.g., Böhm, Ruth, & Schramm, 2016; Boulton, 2012; Greitemeyer, Agthe, Turner, & Gschwendtner, 2012; Greitemeyer & Osswald, 2011; Guéguen, Jacob, & Lamy, 2010; Jin & Li, 2017; Lapierre & Farrar, 2018; Li & Jin, 2014; Liu, Teng, Lan, Zhang, & Yao, 2015; Ruth, 2016) and meta-analytic interpretations (e.g., Fischer, Greitemeyer, Kastenmüller, Vogrincic, & Sauer, 2011). This manuscript is designed to elaborate the current state of the GLM and to serve as the most complete description to date.

4.1 Short-Term Learning Processes: Overview and Detailed Views

The general overview of the short-term model is shown in Figure 6. The timing of this figure is intentionally vague, although it is assumed that all parts could be completed within seconds or minutes.

4.1.1 Inputs

The GLM starts from the assumption that actors exist within an environment, and that both the person and the environment can influence any given learning opportunity. The *person factors* include all aspects of a person at a moment in time, including all prior learning, genetic predisposition, personality traits, beliefs and attitudes, mood, sex, short- and long-term goals, motivation, and attentional resources. That is, at any given moment, you are a combination of immediate states, primed concepts, long-term traits, and your biological and learned history. You may (or may not) have specific goals, and you may direct your attention to focus on particular aspects of your environment. The *situation factors* include all of the information and affordances available in the environment at any given moment. These include the physical environment, other potential social actors in the environment (along with their current states, traits, and motivations), the

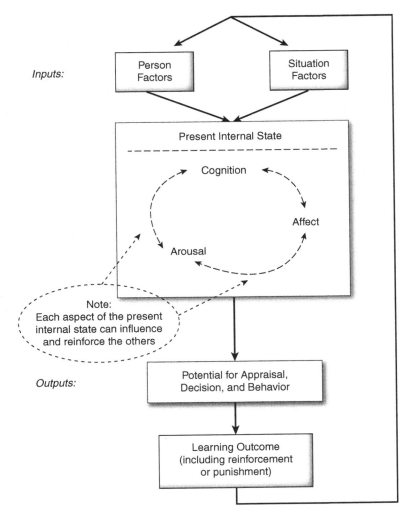

Figure 6 Simplified view of the short-term GLM model

history of the situation to that point, and all of the information that exists to be detected by an organism in the environment.

The short-term overview model (Figure 6) notes that aspects of the person and the environmental situation interact to influence the person's present internal state. At this simplified level, the present internal state is oversimplified to note that we have thoughts, feelings, and physiological reactions, each of which may reinforce or condition the others.

Figures 7a and 7b display the processes that can occur serially and in parallel within the first few seconds of any learning encounter.

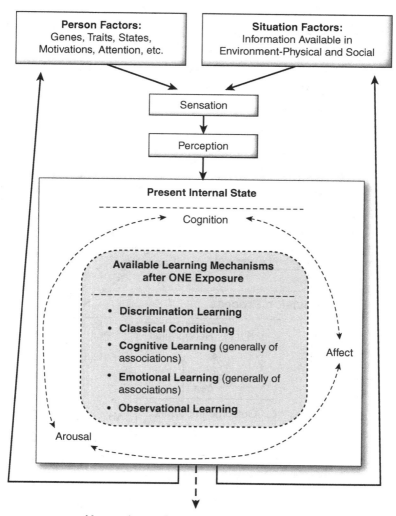

Figure 7a Detailed single-encounter GLM model: Early processes and feedback

4.1.2 Sensation and Perception

Organisms have evolved sensory organs to detect information in the environment relevant to that organism. The first stage of informational input is *sensation*, defined as stimulation of one or more of our senses (e.g., auditory, visual, tactile). *Perception* serves as an immediate product of the situation and the person, which is usually defined as an active cognitive process of making sense of sensations or making meaning of them (e.g., Neisser, 1967). We can perceive

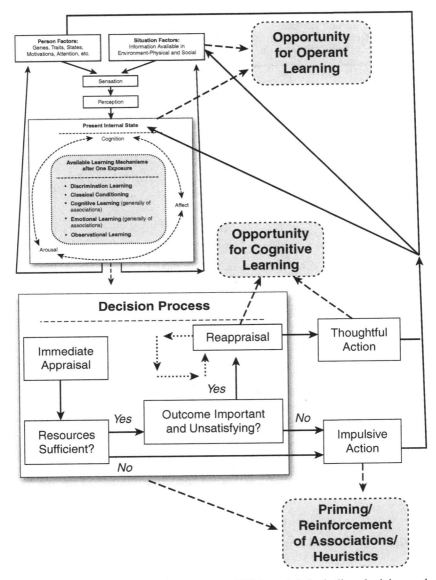

Figure 7b Full detailed single-encounter GLM model, including decision and outcome processes. Note that the early processes (top-left part of the figure) are the same as in Figure 7a

many things directly (e.g., Gibson, 1979), sometimes called perceiving to learn, but we also learn to perceive. Perception can benefit from prior knowledge or experience. We therefore perceive using both bottom-up and top-down processes. In the GLM, this top-down aspect is represented by the input from the person in a given situation. In a learning situation, individuals gather information in the environment and summon relevant knowledge structures to help process and operate upon that information.

Several types of learning can occur immediately at this stage (Figure 7a). A single perception of an object, event, or stimulus (external or internal) could result in

- discrimination, although this is not highly likely with a single perception. It would require that the features salient to the learner at that moment are detectably different from the features of anything to which it might be compared, or if the features are made to be salient;
- classical conditioning, if some reflex was triggered at the same time that the learner was perceiving something to which the reflexive behavior could be associated (e.g., seeing a white rat while simultaneously being scared by a loud noise);
- cognitive learning of associations, if two percepts or concepts are perceived to go together. Advertising often relies on this form of learning, especially because people often only glance at an advertisement for a second or two (e.g., seeing the words "Coca-Cola – Open happiness" or "M&Ms melt in your mouth, not in your hands");
- emotional learning of associations, whereby a percept/concept can be connected to an emotion. Advertising uses this approach even more than cognitive learning of associations, as when the tag line "A diamond is forever" is paired with a romantic and warm picture of attractive people in love; and
- observational learning, if some behavior in the environment is attended to. For example, seeing someone eat with chopsticks immediately teaches that it can be done, even if it isn't clear exactly how.

All of these types of learning can happen very quickly within what the simplified Figure 6 displays as the present internal state – the set of cognitions, feelings, and physiological arousal that may be primed by the interaction of the person and the situation. Nonetheless, there is no necessity for anything to be learned. Individuals may engage in the ongoing activity through automatic responding, or they may pay no attention, or they may be so engaged in their own thoughts that the learning opportunity is missed. This detailed view, however, helps to demonstrate what can be learned in a very brief period of time. Any changes to thoughts, feelings, or arousal, however, can immediately feed back into the set of person and environmental variables. For example, if I insult you, your heart rate increases, and you may feel hurt and think angry thoughts. You might associate negative feelings with the sight of me (classical conditioning), or you might learn a new insult (observational and cognitive learning). The changes to your thoughts, feelings, and arousal change you, including your attention, motivations, and which concepts are primed, which could in turn influence how future events are perceived. Your face may flush and your body language may change, which provides new information in the environment for others to react to, feeding back into a new cycle.

After the present internal state has been influenced, the person may have an opportunity to appraise the situation and respond (Figure 7b). Depending on both the situational variables that are present and the person's motivations and available resources, the initial appraisal may be automatic or thoughtful. If the situation demands a fast response or the outcome is not sufficiently important to warrant careful consideration, the appraisal is likely to be made hastily (e.g., via an impulsive behavioral response) or automatically, based on heuristics (e.g., the *availability* heuristic - judging the frequency of an event by how readily it comes to mind). If the individual has the cognitive resources and time to reappraise the situation and possible actions, a thoughtful action (which could still be based on heuristic biases, and is not necessarily a "better" response) will result. Within this decision process are additional opportunities for learning.

If the actor has the time, motivation, and the cognitive resources necessary to reappraise, the reappraisal process itself may lead to cognitive learning (Figure 7b), as the actor considers the connections between ideas and likely operant outcomes of each option. If the actor takes a thoughtful action based on the reappraisal, the thoughts can reinforce the cognitive concepts that led to that action. Any associations and heuristics (which may have been learned previously or in the immediately prior present internal state) may be primed or reinforced by the decision process, especially if an impulsive action is taken based on heuristic processing. For example, if I insult you, a cognitive script could be activated whereby when provoked you should retaliate. If you do, it serves as a practice trial reinforcing the script.

Once an action is taken (including no response, which is an action), the action feeds back into the person factors, the situational factors, and the actor's present internal state (Figure 7b). Both the situation and the present internal state provide opportunities for operant learning. Others in the environment may respond in a way that is reinforcing or punishing, by which the behaviors chosen by the actor may be shaped. Similarly, the actor may have a response to their own behavior, such as feeling happy or guilty about the action taken. These internal feelings and evaluations can also act as operant reinforcers or punishments.

Each of these opportunities for learning can occur in a single episode, but additional learning opportunities are afforded by multiple exposures to some situation or stimulus (see Figure 8).

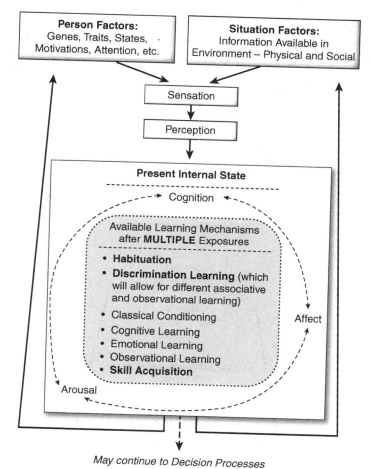

Figure 8 Detailed multiple-encounter GLM model: Early processes

After multiple exposures, the individual may demonstrate habituation to the stimulus. Discrimination learning becomes much more likely with repeated experience, where people can detect finer and finer differences and similarities between stimuli and categorize them differently. After the differences have been detected, both associative and observational learning mechanisms are enhanced. In addition, repetition can begin the acquisition of skills.

4.2 Long-Term Processes

Repeated exposure to any experience can lead to different long-term effects. As knowledge structures and emotions are repeatedly primed, associated with various internal and external stimuli, and reinforced or punished, they become better developed, more easily accessible, and more interconnected with other knowledge structures. The GLM proposes four categories of long-term effects: perceptual and cognitive constructs, cognitive-behavioral constructs, cognitive-emotional constructs, and emotional constructs (Figure 9).

4.2.1 Perceptual and Cognitive Constructs

The first category includes perceptual and cognitive constructs such as the development and reinforcement of perceptual or expectancy schemata

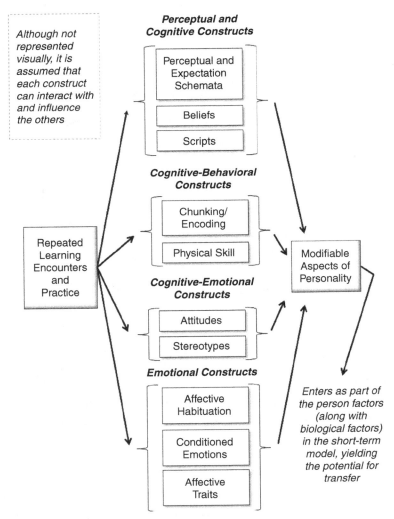

Figure 9 Long-term GLM model

(Kirsh, 1998), beliefs (Fontana & Beckerman, 2004; Huesmann & Guerra, 1997), and behavioral scripts (Anderson et al., 2004). These effects are hypothesized to be learned from repeated exposure to or experience with relevant situations. For example, many violent video games require the player to be constantly on alert for attackers, and this practice being hypervigilant for aggression appears to increase hostile attribution bias – a perceptual schema by which others' ambiguous actions are perceived to be of hostile intent. Similarly, being reinforced repeatedly for behaving aggressively in violent video games appears to predict increases in normative beliefs about aggression – a cognitive belief that it is acceptable to behave aggressively when provoked (Gentile, Li, Khoo, Prot, & Anderson, 2014).

4.2.2 Cognitive-Behavioral Constructs

Other examples of extended practice have emerged from the study of experts and novices. All experts begin as novices and it is of scientific interest to understand how the change occurs. Modern coaches have refined the adage "practice makes perfect" to "perfect practice makes perfect." That is, a tennis player would be coached to correct the mechanics of a swing and then practice the new stroke repeatedly so that it becomes habitual, automatic, confident, and reliable, despite changing situations and stresses.

This description implies that expertise can occur by repeatedly performing that skill – a behavioral process. But improving expertise also requires cognitive restructuring. For example, an 18-month study of a college student's organization of memory for digits showed improvement from the typical digit span of seven to seventy-nine (Chase & Ericsson, 1981; Ericsson, Chase, & Faloon, 1980). To get beyond the 7 ± 2 magic number (Miller, 1956), this student drew on his expertise as a long-distance runner and began to chunk the digits into running times for various races: 3492 became 3 minutes, 49.2 seconds, a near world record for the mile. Other digits were chunked into ages of runners. He perfected this technique over 75 days and increased his digit span to between twenty-five and thirty (4 chunked digits $\times$ 7 ± 2 equals about 28). To go beyond this, he invented various hierarchies, such as world record times, average times, and practice times. Continued practice and restructuring yielded an amazingly high level of expertise.

Some theorists have argued that learning of a complex skill (such as learning to drive a car or to type) involves three stages: (1) a cognitive stage where the learner must first learn and remember lists of instructions about what and when to do things, (2) an associative stage, where the cognitive/semantic memory is supplanted or enhanced by more direct and nonconceptual learning of the sequence of movements needed, and finally (3) an autonomous stage, where the skill is automatic and free from conscious control (Anderson, 1982). Regardless of whether all skills go through such stages as they are learned, it is clear that skill development is not solely behavioral. Furthermore, although deliberate practice is related to skill performance, it accounts for less variance than one might expect (i.e., 26 percent of variance in games, 21 percent in music, and 18 percent in sports performance; Macnamara, Hambrick, & Oswald, 2014). Individual differences, motivations, and situational and task factors must also be involved in why so few people become experts.

Nonetheless, once one has become an expert, there are distinct differences between experts and novices in memory, organization, and rate of processing information in such diverse fields as chess (Chase & Simon, 1973), music (Halpern & Bower, 1982), mathematics (Hunter, 1978), and reading (Bloom, 1986). We have therefore added expertise through extended practice as a separate domain of the long-term GLM, with reciprocal influences on and from each of the other domains.

4.2.3 Cognitive-Emotional Constructs

The third category includes constructs that link cognitive and affective aspects such as attitudes and stereotypes. One example already described was how playing a game involving the fighting of terrorists fostered negative attitudes toward Arabs and Muslims more generally (Saleem & Anderson, 2013). Attitudes, however, can also be changed in ways that are beneficial. One research team created a video game to change attitudes toward dating violence, with some results suggesting that it not only created greater awareness (discrimination learning) but also changed attitudes (Bowen et al., 2014). Repeated play would likely strengthen these results.

When people (especially therapists) speak of the necessity of "getting in touch with your feelings," we suspect that they are trying to teach people that cognition and emotion are or can be linked. Furthermore, this relation is bidirectional in that (1) we can experience an emotion and then analyze and manipulate it, or (2) we can plan and practice how to recognize and work with an emotion before it happens. Anger management and mindfulness are examples of practices that recognize that learning can influence cognitive-emotional constructs.

4.2.4 Emotional Constructs

As shown in Figure 9, repeated exposure is also hypothesized to lead to long-term influences on emotional constructs such as affective habituation (e.g., associating media violence with fun and excitement), conditioned emotions (e.g., desensitization to real-life violence following media violence exposure), and affective traits (e.g., the development of trait anger for habitual violent video game players; Bushman & Huesmann, 2006).

4.2.5 Example of Long-Term Learning Processes

One simple example of the multiple long-term effects resulting from these interrelated processes comes from considering the design of "loot" systems within many violent video games. After killing an enemy, often one can loot the body and receive a random reward. These rewards are usually of minor value, but occasionally they provide a large benefit (e.g., a powerful new weapon). By establishing a connection between the cognitive concepts of, say, "kill the bad guy" and "receive reward," the repeated learning trials develop a knowledge structure associating the two. The most obvious outcome of this linkage is the development of a behavioral script (kill enemy, potentially receive reward, repeat).

This variable reinforcement strategy supports maintaining a behavior. Therefore, one keeps practicing, and additional long-term effects occur. Learners develop a positive association with sitting in front of screens (conditioned emotion) as the space and posture are also part of that new knowledge structure. The physical skills to play are refined as expertise is gained, and information becomes easier to chunk – that is, one can get more information from the screen more quickly and hold it in working memory. Attitudes toward video game playing (and consequently, violence) also become more positive (or negative attitudes diminish) and beliefs may change (the belief that aggressive responses to provocations are normative). These processes are continually reinforced with each short-term learning cycle occurring for each enemy killed.

4.3 Implications

A fundamental quality of the GLM is that it recognizes that learning is dynamic, occurring on multiple levels and through a variety of routes, some in parallel with each other, and others only serially. As an example, although much has been written about different types of associative learning, very little has been noted about discrimination learning that must occur prior to it. If everything sounds like a bell, then saying that one is a handbell, one a singing bowl, and one a gong does not help. The names cannot be associated with different sounds until the sounds are discriminably different to you.

That said, the opposite side of this equation has generated a lot of research – that of generalization of responses. This was noted by Pavlov, Watson, and many other early learning theorists (c.f., Razran, 1949). After being conditioned to fear a white rat, the infant Little Albert also now showed fear to a white rabbit, a Santa Claus beard, a brown rabbit, and even a medium-sized brown dog (Watson & Rayner, 1920). Stimulus generalization is evidence of a lack of discrimination. The important issue is that by including each of the domain-specific learning mechanisms into a general metatheoretic model, we can make and test more precise predictions than perhaps were previously possible.

Because the GLM integrates multiple domain-specific theories (such as classical and operant conditioning), the specifics are not novel. Although each specific theory can successfully describe how learning occurs within a given context, it is often the case that multiple learning mechanisms may be applied in any given real-world (or laboratory) context. The GLM can provide novel testable hypotheses, however, by depicting how some types of learning may depend on other learning mechanisms occurring first, or how multiple learning mechanisms may interact to improve (or hinder) learning.

5 The Processes of Learning and Forgetting

Humans have multiple mechanisms through which learning can occur. There are, however, some general processes that are relevant across the different specific mechanisms. Learning of almost anything follows a predictable pattern – an S-shaped learning curve (Figure 10). There is a negatively accelerating acquisition of skill or knowledge from initial trials to close-to-perfect performance at asymptote. The slope of the curve depends on the difficulty or complexity of the content or skill, which interacts with individual differences in learners.

There are individual differences among people in their speed of learning and/or intelligence. Nonetheless, the major difference is often their prior knowledge, or readiness. Those who are adequately prepared for the new material – because they have mastered the prerequisites and can see their relevance to the present task (a transfer problem) – can immediately acquire new material. Those for whom such prerequisite knowledge is absent will languish for a while in the lower portion of the learning curve (inexperience). If the prerequisites have been mislearned or are otherwise inaccurate, then progress in learning is further confounded with the need to correct or unlearn these prior misconceptions (an example of negative transfer due to proactive interference).

With sufficient practice, progress resembles the S-shaped curve: progressively fewer errors on a piano piece or achieving a higher score in a game. As performance approaches criterion, it levels out and, if the criterion was set sufficiently high, we can say that *initial mastery* was achieved (Gentile & Lalley, 2003).

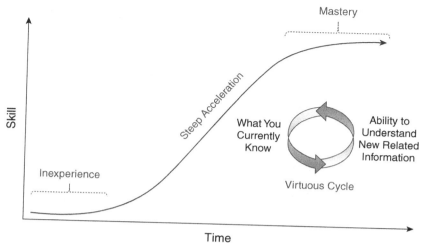

Figure 10 The S-shaped learning curve

Forgetting begins within hours or days after initial mastery. So why learn at all? Because *relearning is faster* (Ebbinghaus, 1885/1964). That is, there is a considerable saving in time or trials to relearn after the material originally learned to criterion is forgotten. Each relearning trial, called overlearning, adds significantly to recall (Krueger, 1929; Postman, 1962).

Learning and forgetting can therefore be seen to occur in various episodes or phases (Figure 11). Phase 1, that of initial or original learning, includes the readiness (prerequisites) component, learning to mastery, and subsequent forgetting. Phase 2 and beyond are all cases of overlearning, which include relearning to criterion and forgetting (recall should continually improve from phase to phase).

Figure 11 represents the learning/forgetting process in close-to-optimal conditions because learners took the time and effort to master the material initially and were brought to criterion on each relearning episode. Relearning is faster, and a great deal is retained. Under such optimal conditions, there are also other indirect positive effects of overlearning. Each relearning episode, for example, occurs under slightly different conditions, creating additional cues for recall. Each rehearsal allows the material to be reconsidered and reorganized with new examples. Such recognizing may therefore not only improve memory but also facilitate transfer.

If, in contrast, learners do not master the material initially, then there is no overlearning and little or no savings in relearning or improvements in memory (Figure 12). Even when there is the opportunity for relearning, it is likely that

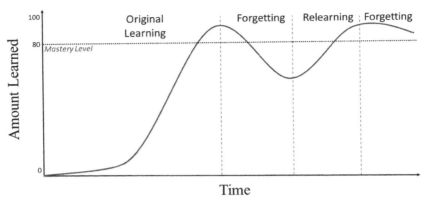

Figure 11 Phases of learning, forgetting, and relearning/overlearning when the original learning was adequate (mastery)

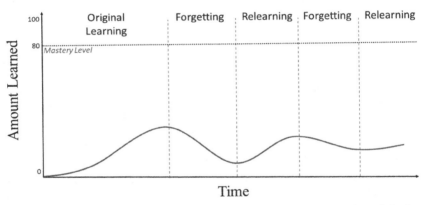

Figure 12 Phases of learning, forgetting, and relearning when the original learning was inadequate (nonmastery)

the new learning will not surpass the original amount of learning, because students will think they previously knew enough, or they recognize it would take a lot of effort to go beyond what they already did. This belief interacts with the emotional and behavioral levels of learning, where with each new relearning episode (in, say, math) learners will recall that they did not learn this material before, that they are not very good at this, and – eventually – they will give up trying. Learned helplessness will have set in (Dweck & Licht, 1980; Gentile & Monaco, 1988; Seligman, 1975).

Video game makers appear to understand this. Most video games are designed with mastery and automaticity in mind. When knowledge and skills have developed to the point of mastery, continued practice allows for over-learning, in which knowledge and skills become automatized and solidified in memory. This allows the learner to free up cognitive resource to have more ability to learn and connect new concepts and information.

The complexity and difficulty are both carefully sequenced so that players are never completely overwhelmed, but so that they can master necessary skills for later levels. At the beginning of many games, for example, there are "training modes" in which players are slowly exposed to each of the controls used in the game. If players are not yet able to continue on to the next stage in a game, they are often allowed to replay levels until the necessary skills have been mastered.

5.1 Learning Rate and Memory

One might expect fast learners to remember more of what they learned for such reasons as better mastery of prerequisites, better learning strategies, or higher IQ. Nonetheless, when equated on amount learned, fast and slow learners forget at the same rate (Gentile, Monaco, Iheozor-Ejiofor, Ndu, & Ogbonaya, 1982; Gregory & Bunch, 1959; Underwood, 1954). In other words, it is the amount of learning, not the rate of learning, that accounts for what is recalled.

Textbooks have traditionally divided memory processes into three types: sensory, short-term, and long-term. An after-image phenomenon provides a prototype for sensory memory, such as our experience when a lit match is waved in a darkened room, where we can continue to "see" it for about 2 seconds after it has gone out (Neisser, 1967).

Short-term memory gives us another 20–60 seconds to attend to, organize, rehearse, and store (in long-term memory) incoming information so that it is accessible later. The short-term store is about 7 ± 2 unrelated items (Miller, 1956). By *chunking* these unrelated items into meaningful subsets, we can, for example, turn eight items (1 7 7 6 1 4 9 2) into two (1776 and 1492).

Long-term memory is whatever remains after being attended to, rehearsed, or organized during the short term. This implies that perhaps there may not really be a short-term store at all; rather, that the difference between what remains and what is lost from exposure to new material is how much time is available and how well the learner is able to process the material (e.g., Bugelski, 1979; Ellis & Hunt, 1993). We therefore turn to another way to examine these processes.

5.2 Encoding, Storage, and Retrieval

How does new information that decays quickly become relatively permanent? The brief answer is that it must be encoded (recognized, chunked, categorized, labeled, or rendered meaningful in some way). Once stored, the material is available, but whether it is accessible depends on the cues that were encoded along with the information. Tulving and Thompson (1973) called this the *encoding specificity principle*. Figure 13 provides a flow diagram to illustrate the interactions of encoding, storage, and retrieval functions as described.

By this argument, what is usually considered memory failure ("I can't recall his name") is most often a failure during encoding to rehearse or associate cues with the person ("Where did I meet him?"). Such memory problems also depend on what and how much there is to be learned before and after (e.g., how many other people you are meeting), which is a problem of proactive and retroactive interference (discussed later).

5.3 Organization, Elaboration, and Imagery

Cues and organizations can facilitate recall even when interference occurs. Tulving and Psotka (1971) gave students from one to six categorical word lists of four words each (e.g., tree, flower, weed, bush, and mother, uncle, brother, cousin). They had three practice trials with each list, in different random orders but within category. After all lists were learned, they were asked to recall as many of the words as possible (noncued condition). In another treatment, the cued condition, students were given an answer sheet with category labels (e.g., plants or relationships). Students who learned only one list recalled about 70 percent of the words in the noncued condition and about 75 percent in the cued condition. Students who learned six lists could recall only 40 percent of list 1 without cues, but 70 percent of list 1 with cues. The category cues almost eliminated the retroactive interference effects of the other lists.

The lists in this study, though not labeled up front, were categorized for the learners. Many of life's learning experiences are more random, requiring learners to supply their own organization: perhaps alphabetical, by category, or some other subjective organization. With some of such subjective organization at encoding, memory is significantly improved (e.g., Ericsson, Chase, & Faloon, 1980; Shuell, 1969; Tulving, 1962), perhaps most easily accomplished via verbal or visual elaboration.

Verbal and visual elaborations may be independent, as Paivio's dual-coding theory suggests (Paivio, 1991), but they can also interact. Imagery elaboration techniques tend to be better than verbal techniques, which are better than simple rote learning. Thus, manipulating objects and drawing graphs – that is, active learning processes – will likely produce better recall than dealing with the same material in a verbal or symbolic way. It remains to be determined,

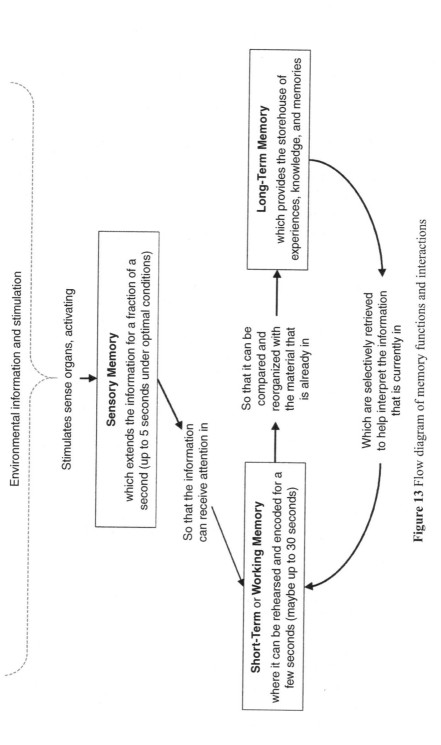

Environmental information and stimulation

Stimulates sense organs, activating

Sensory Memory
which extends the information for a fraction of a second (up to 5 seconds under optimal conditions)

So that the information can receive attention in

So that it can be compared and reorganized with the material that is already in

Long-Term Memory
which provides the storehouse of experiences, knowledge, and memories

Which are selectively retrieved to help interpret the information that is currently in

Short-Term or **Working Memory**
where it can be rehearsed and encoded for a few seconds (maybe up to 30 seconds)

Figure 13 Flow diagram of memory functions and interactions

however, how similar the active engagement in video games is to other active learning techniques.

5.4 Massed and Distributed Practice

How new material is practiced matters, as we have seen, but perhaps in different ways for original learning and long-term memory. Bloom and Shuell (1981) examined high school students learning English-French vocabulary equivalents. Half the students practiced lists in 10-minute exercises on 3 successive days, while the other half practiced all three 10-minute exercises in succession on the same day. Immediately after the third exercise, both groups were tested, with no significant difference between them. Four days later, both groups were surprised with a retention test with the distributed and massed practice groups retaining 89 percent and 69 percent, respectively, of their performance scores on the immediate test. This finding – that there is little or no difference between massed and distributed practice on original learning, but a large and significant effect on long-term memory – is well-documented (Cain & Willey, 1939; Ebbinghaus, 1885/1964; Reynolds & Glaser, 1964). Combining distributed practice with imagery techniques also appears to have independent and cumulative effects (Baehre & Gentile, 1991).

In the earliest phases of learning many tasks, however, massed practice may facilitate getting past the bracketed portion named "Inexperience" in Figure 10. But distributed sessions provide opportunities to practice retrieval, to recognize, encode and store material for future access, to practice retrieval again, and so on. This is what subject matter experts do and, likely, one important reason that their memories for their subject show little dissipation over time – a stage called *permastore* because it is available for the next 25 years or longer (Bahrick, 1984).

5.5 Reproductive or Reconstructive Memories

By all the evidence presented, it seems clear that what is remembered is more likely to be constructed at encoding and then *reconstructed* at retrieval than it is to be *reproduced* as in a photograph or rote repetition. This is perhaps most true of learning from prose, interpreting stories, recalling incidents, and the like (Bartlett, 1932).

Consider the task of recalling a childhood outing with your family or what you were doing when the twin towers came down on 9/11. Many people swear they can reproduce what they were doing where and with whom. Unfortunately, it is extremely difficult to confirm these reports and, when evidence can be found, it often contradicts the assertions.

A second problem is that as time passes, we are not likely to be able to discern what actually happened (our original learning) from our subsequent reconstructions of what happened (retrieval, reorganization, retelling/reexperiencing, and storage after distributed practice). In addition, during these subsequent conversations, we are particularly vulnerable to others' suggestions, including deliberately misleading suggestions that can make "a lie become memory's truth," as Loftus (1992) phrased it (Ceci, DeSimone Leichtman, Putnick, & Nightingale, 1993).

5.6 Metacognition

Adopting better memory strategies to diagnose errors is facilitated by skill in monitoring one's own cognitive processes. Metacognitive processes include thinking about your thinking, monitoring the effectiveness of your learning strategies, searching our memories for cues which might help recall, knowing how and when a certain strategy might be useful, and, in general, providing an executive function to our cognitive processes (Flavell, 1979; Keeney, Cannizzo, & Flavell, 1967; Pressley, Borkowski, & O'Sullivan, 1984).

Metacognitive development is not as inevitable as physical maturation, however. Students often develop "illusions of learning" or false confidence in their cognitive strategies. For example, many college students believe that rereading material several times improves learning more than attempting to retrieve via tests (Geller et al., 2018), that cramming for a test is more beneficial than distributing their studying (Carpenter, 2017), and that viewing colorful images alongside reading materials improves their comprehension (Carpenter & Geller, 2020) – none of which are accurate. Nonetheless, it does seem possible to "inoculate" students against these powerful illusions of learning and improve their metacognitive skills (Carpenter, Witherby, & Tauber, 2020). Continued research in this area is promising, therefore, for theories of intelligence as well as for learning and memory.

5.7 Experts versus Novices and the Role of Knowledge

Extending the findings of DeGroot (1965, 1966), Chase and Simon (1973) compared chess masters with experienced players and novices on their memory for chess pieces on a board. They did this by giving a 5-second glimpse of a chess board and then asking them to recreate what they recalled on an empty board, with several trials to allow and score improvement, if any. Half of the displays came from either the midpoint or ending of a real game, and half consisted of the same number of chess pieces placed randomly on the board. There was a positive relation between skill level and memory for the pieces from the real games, but no difference between the masters and less experienced players on the pieces placed randomly.

The implications of this research are both straightforward and profound: the differences between experts and novices are not due to better memories in general, but due to (1) more domain-specific knowledge, (2) more automatized strategies for chunking and encoding new information (i.e., schemata), and (3) better metacognitive processes, including heuristics, for estimating and monitoring their strategies. These arise from thousands of hours of distributed practice solving problems in a variety of contexts and conditions, thus making their memories relatively impervious to interference from intervening tasks and less reliant on specific algorithms or a "one best method" mentality (Charness, 1976).

The advances we make occur because we automatize much of the process. Whereas the beginning reader must focus on each letter, the skilled reader focuses on the ideas, plots, or style because the mechanics of reading are automatic. Skilled gamers, likewise, see and hear more when they play a video game, because they automatically recognize patterns and can therefore focus their attention on anomalies or unique features.

Differences in prior knowledge lengthen the period in the "inexperience" portion of Figure 10, while sufficient prior knowledge facilitates the beginning and slope of acquisition. In literacy scores, for example, children with poor vocabulary and reading skills fall progressively further behind and, by fourth grade, are still learning to read while their more advanced peers are reading to learn (Chall & Jacobs, 2003). Until one reaches a sufficient level of expertise in a given domain, practice is often rote drudgery. "What's necessary is sustained practice. . . . This kind of practice past the point of mastery is necessary to meet any of these three important goals of instruction: acquiring facts and knowledge, learning skills, or becoming an expert" (Willingham, 2004, p. 31).

5.8 Transfer

Transfer can be defined as "the ability to use previously learned skills or knowledge in settings or on problems different from the original learning, including the capacity to distinguish when and where these learnings are appropriate" (Gentile, 2000, p. 13). It therefore presupposes prior learning as well as adequate memory for what was learned.

Theories about transfer have evolved over the past century. This is not the place to describe them in detail, but the interested reader can examine identical elements theory (Thorndike, 1923; Thorndike & Woodworth, 1901), critical positions such as Judd (1908), interference theory (e.g., Underwood, 1957), and situated cognition theory, which argued that what comes to be known is context-specific and largely determined by *how* it is learned (Brown, Collins, & Duguid, 1989; Singley & Anderson, 1989). Barnett and Ceci (2002) summarized and classified transfer based on how similar (near or far) it is to the original learning. Sadly, the accumulated research shows little evidence for learners' ability to spontaneously transfer what they have learned.

Given the paucity of strong evidence of transfer from the classroom to other contexts, it is surprising to realize that much of the research on video game effects can be interpreted as demonstrating "far" transfer. As noted in Section 2.2, for example, repeated playing of prosocial video games seems to generalize and transfer to greater helpful and cooperative behaviors in the real world – that is, to situations that share almost no characteristics that are similar to those in the video games.

Salomon and Perkins (1989) suggested two roads to transfer, based on the existing evidence about learning and memory:

- The low road: "much practice in a large variety of situations, leading to a high level of mastery and automaticity"
- The high road: "deliberate mindful abstraction of a principle"

Gentile (2000) derived the following eight recommendations from a century of research. Learners must (1) develop a rich knowledge base and automatize basic skills; (2) practice multiple strategies to avoid a "one-best-way" mentality or perceptual set; (3) recall and activate their prerequisite knowledge in the target situation; (4) identify underlying principles and recognize their relevance in diverse problems or tasks; (5) monitor their own comprehension, along with using other metacognitive processes; and (6) continually reorganize their knowledge and skills in different social contexts. Finally, (7) the curricula should be so sequenced that each unit reinforces, reviews, and incorporates material from previous units, as well as anticipates subsequent units; and (8) since learning is contextualized, training-to-transfer contexts should be structured accordingly. Ironically, these recommendations seem to be incorporated in video games much better than in schools.

5.9 Moderators of Learning

In any given situation where learning is possible, not everyone will learn the same amount or even the same specifics. Multiple factors can moderate what gets attended to, how the current situation interacts with prior knowledge, and how the brain encodes and retains information. Some examples are described next.

5.9.1 Emotion and Stress

Emotional states can increase vigilance, alter what one attends to, and change the brain's neurochemistry to influence memory retention. As an example, participants learned words in pairs, where some of the words were emotionally charged words, such as kiss, rape, and money, whereas others were neutral (Kleinsmith & Kaplan, 1963). At immediate recall, neutral words were remembered better than emotional words. When tested a week later, however, participants recalled the emotional words better than the neutral words. Emotions can, therefore, moderate what is learned and recalled in ways that may not be immediately straightforward and are related to various brain and hormonal processes that are beyond the scope of this discussion.

5.9.2 Motivation

As one acquires, or fails to acquire, efficacy in new endeavors, they also solidify beliefs about their self-efficacy (Bandura, 1986). If your experiences convince you that you are not very good at math or video games, then those beliefs will likely affect your willingness to participate in those activities. If asked why, you may respond, "I was never good in math" or "video games are a waste of time." These excuses, called attributions (e.g., Weiner, 1974, 2010), are personal causal explanations for why you would not attempt those activities. Such beliefs are commonly associated with learned helplessness, in which learners appear to save face and give up before even trying (Dweck, 1986; Dweck & Licht, 1980; Gentile & Monaco, 1988). In contrast are attitudes and beliefs that accompany the development of competence in various arenas, namely, self-efficacy, in which new hurdles are considered as worthy challenges. In such ways attitudes and beliefs provide motivation (or lack thereof) for probably any phase or type of learning.

Self-Determination Theory also describes three motivational needs: autonomy (a feeling of agency and control), competence (a need for personal growth and mastery), and relatedness (a need for meaningful relations to feel connected and valued by others). Intrinsic motivation increases when the activity meets one or more of these needs (Ryan & Deci, 2000). Several studies have demonstrated how video games are excellent at meeting all three of these needs, which can at least partially account for why gamers are able to continue learning and playing despite frustrations (Bender & Gentile, 2020; Ryan, Rigby, & Przybylski, 2006).

5.9.3 Level of Processing

When learning, qualitative differences in how the material is analyzed at the time of encoding can change the amount that is learned. For example, when studying a list of words, attending to surface characteristics (whether the words are in capital or lowercase letters) resulted in poorer learning than when attending to the meaning of the words (Craik & Tulving, 1975). Furthermore, when the memory test itself is designed to match the level of processing used at encoding, performance is enhanced (Challis, Velichkovsky, & Craik, 1996).

5.9.4 Developmental Stages

Hierarchies of developmental stages imply that children at lower stages are probably not ready to tackle tasks that require reasoning or skills at higher stages (e.g., Flavell, 1971; Flavell, Friedrichs, & Hoyt, 1970). If so, they fall in the "inexperience" portion of the S-shaped learning curve (Figure 10), and will take longer to begin to show progress than children who are at the appropriate developmental stage. If they have a developmental delay, they may take longer or may not be able to master a given learning task.

At the higher stages, formal operations, logic, and metacognitive processes are possible, which enable children to organize their own knowledge for increased memory capacity and transfer on the road to expertise. In these ways, developmental stages are predictive of learning success. For example, dual process models of decision-making suggest that decisions can be guided by a faster, heuristic-based, habitual set of largely automatic responses, or by a slower, more deliberative and goal-directed set of processes (Kahneman, 2011). A study of children, adolescents, and adults found that all age groups would tend to repeat choices that initially produced rewards, but the ability to mentally construct a model to enhance success only began to emerge in adolescence and was strongest in adults (Decker, Otto, Daw, & Hartley, 2016). Other developmental studies have found that after the initial S-shaped curve of learning, there can be more changes in the curve with development (such as N-shaped curves, where learning occurs, then what looks like forgetting, but then it increases again with development rather than with retraining; Rakison & Yermolayeva, 2011). The ways in which age may predict how the different learning mechanisms/processes occur independently and together, in conjunction with various potential moderators, is a fruitful area for future research.

5.9.5 Proactive and Retroactive Interference

As one begins to learn something new, the new information can be more or less difficult to learn based on what one already knows and what happens after the learning session. Previously known information likely affects how new information is attended to and encoded to facilitate learning or provide proactive interference. Interference is usually considered to be harmful to memory, as when a prior experience makes it more difficult to learn new materials (e.g., learning measurements in feet and inches first can make it harder to learn the metric system). Nonetheless, prior learning can facilitate learning of new material, such as when learning a mnemonic technique makes it easier to learn and remember names. Likewise, memory consolidation and retrieval of previously learned material can also be hampered due to information that was learned after it, known as retroactive interference (Underwood, 1957). Similarly, retroactive facilitation is also possible, where subsequent experiences make it easier to relearn or recall previously learned material, such as when learning the biological classification system helps us to categorize and understand the animals we learned differently as children (e.g., how birds are modern dinosaurs).

5.9.6 Context and Mood

The context in which we learn something can affect how well it is remembered. As noted by Godden and Baddeley (1975), memory is better when tested in the same context that the words were learned. Their study of verbal learning on land or underwater was extended in a video game study, where participants were randomly assigned to one of two contexts – being on a ship or being in a city environment (Busching & Krahé, 2013). If they had played the violent game on a ship, they had easier access to aggressive thoughts if they were primed with ship-related words rather than city-related words (and vice versa for those who had played in the city context when they were primed with city-related words). Therefore, contextual cues that we might assume are irrelevant to what is being learned may also influence learning and memory.

Similar to situation context effects on learning and memory, one's mental or emotional state can affect learning and memory. For example, one study asked participants to memorize lists of words, which included positive, neutral, and negative words. Participants' moods were then manipulated to feel either happy or sad. Following this mood manipulation, participants remembered more words with meanings that matched their induced mood than words that did not (Teasdale & Russell, 1983).

5.9.7 Social Identity

Social identity might also be considered a type of context effect. Seeing something as relevant (or not) to the self can influence attention, encoding, and practice. Additionally, even desiring something to be relevant can influence learning. For example, boys who wished they were like an aggressive character in a violent video game increased their willingness to behave aggressively in a subsequent task (Konijn, Bijvank, & Bushman, 2007).

5.9.8 Consolidation Disruptors

Sleep appears to be essential for the consolidation of learning, and perhaps more so for perceptual and motor learning than for cognitive learning (Siegel, 2001; Walker & Stickgold, 2004). It is worth noting, perhaps, that although we are discussing each of these moderators independently, they can interact. For example, one experimental study had participants learn lists of words in one of two rooms that were different in terms of size, odor, and background music. They were tested in either the same room or a different one after either a day of wakefulness or a night of sleep. If they had slept, the room context effect was reduced – people could remember more words in the different room (Cairney, Durrant, Musgrove, & Lewis, 2011).

Several other variables can disrupt the consolidation of learning. These include alcohol, drugs, electroconvulsive shocks, or distractor tasks (Dudai, 2004). Perhaps germane to modern learning contexts, interruptions such as from one's mobile phone can also damage learning and memory (Cutrell, Czerwinski, & Horvitz, 2001).

General health can also affect ability to encode and remember learned information. Diseases and their treatments can affect learning through many processes, including general fatigue or specific side effects.

6 Summary, Implications, and How Video Games Use These Learning Principles

We have attempted a synthesis of diverse aspects of learning and memory. It is indebted to Bandura's (1977, 1986) Social Cognitive Theory. We have followed his example of including behavioral, emotional, personal, and social components interacting in reciprocal determination, and his concern for such practical issues as the effects of models on behavior. We are also deeply indebted to Craig Anderson for first suggesting the creation of a GLM as a possible extension of his General Aggression Model.

Learning is not mechanistic, but dynamic. The model has separate but continually and reciprocally interacting emotional, behavioral, observational, and cognitive components, each subject to a wide range of individual differences within and among these components. Thus emotions, which viscerally are likely associated to people and situations via respondent conditioning, also have behavioral (motivational) and cognitive (conceptual and attitudinal) causes and effects; for example, when you like and feel comfortable at the piano, you are more likely to practice. Behaviors, which can be regulated by consequences (via operant conditioning and/or observational learning), also have emotional and cognitive causes and effects; for example, when you are punished for your efforts at math, you become fearful and either study harder to acquire the required knowledge or decide that this material is beyond you. Cognitive processes, which are likely governed by what you already know and whether you can learn and remember the new material to a level that is useful (i.e., potentially transferrable), also have emotional and behavioral causes and effects; for example, if you are a really good reader and clever with words, you are likely to be praised by others often and feel relaxed and happy when you are reading and writing. Observational learning can be added to any of the aforementioned examples with behavioral (latent or overt), emotional (vicarious or direct), and cognitive components.

There is a long-standing debate in psychology about which of these is primary – the thought, the emotion, or the action? An early account, the James-Lange Theory, argued that when we feel afraid, it is because we run away, not conversely. More recently, the debate centered on whether thoughts or feelings were primary (Lazarus, 1982, 1984; Zajonc, 1980, 1984). Each (as did William James, 1906) moderated their views to concede that whichever comes first the others follow . . . in milliseconds, we presume. It is possible that such questions may someday be answerable, although it is not clear. For example, in one remarkable study, participants were connected to an EEG machine, with another electrode on their finger (Libet, Gleason, Wright, & Pearl, 1983). The electrode on the finger could show exactly when the finger was moved relative to the brain functions needed to move it. Participants were seated in front of an oscilloscope with a quickly moving dial like a clock, and asked to decide when to move their finger. They were also asked to note where the dial was when they made the decision to move their finger. People moved their fingers about 200 ms after "deciding" to move them. This fits with our general experience – we make a conscious decision to do something and then do it shortly after the decision. The fascinating thing about this study is that the researchers could see that the brain ramped up about a half second *before* the person became aware of the "decision." Thus, our brains decide before we know we've decided, or at least before the decision becomes aware to conscious conceptual thought. Thus, disentangling who and what and which type of process is primary may never be easily answered. Therefore, for psychological theorizing it is best, we believe, to assume that emotional, behavioral, observational, and cognitive elements are present and able to interact in every situation.

Two additional implications result from the GLM. First, we can have a great deal of control over what, how much, and how well we learn. We can intentionally engage in practices that can increase our learning, such as repetition, getting sufficient sleep, or distributing practice thoughtfully. This is not a novel implication. The second one, however, may be a little more startling – preventing learning from happening is difficult, if not impossible. Many of these processes occur automatically and without any active participation or intention from the learner. Studies on media effects have emphasized this very point, as people do not usually play video games with an intention to learn anything other than how to play the game or to win. Nonetheless, the brain learns almost effortlessly from anything it encounters, whether intentional or not. Recognizing that the emotional, observational, behavioral, and cognitive types of learning are constantly interacting with each other also implies that a person can be reached in any number of ways, and that the learner can learn multiple things at once without conscious awareness that learning has occurred.

6.1 Exemplary Dimensions of Video Games

Other implications come into clearer focus through various specific components of the theory. For example, how do video games capture and maintain players' interests, motivating them to keep trying despite initial failures? The GLM can be applied to this problem to examine how games are designed to foster learning, even when designers and players do not intend to play to learn.

Games have become increasingly complex and able to adapt to the gamer, which allows them to incorporate several mechanisms relevant to learning, such as varying difficulty levels, reinforcement schedules, paired associations, and specific training modules. Gentile and Gentile (2008) listed seven exemplary dimensions of video game play to effectively teach players, which we state briefly here and then draw out some themes. Games are able to train players easily by (1) having clear objectives, often set at multiple levels of difficulty, which can adapt to the prior knowledge, skills, and pace of learners; (2) providing practice, feedback, and more practice until a mastery criterion is attained; (3) continuing the game beyond initial mastery to provide overlearning; (4) reinforcing developing skills extrinsically with points, better weapons, and so on, and intrinsically with higher levels of competence and the emotional satisfaction (self-efficacy) that arises from competence; (5) embedding all of this in a spiral curriculum that reinforces past learning and prepares for the next challenges; (6) encouraging a close-to-optimal combination of massed and distributed practice; and (7) challenging players to practice their skills on a variety of problems and in a variety of ways and situations, thus increasing the probability of transfer. In addition, if the game includes violence, increasing the levels of violent acts as the game progresses habituates the user into being more tolerant and accepting of such acts.

Finally, these games are marketed as being "cool" and something one must have to fit in with peers. Let's examine some of these aspects in a little more detail.

6.1.1 Pace Matching

Not all people learn at the same pace. Some studies suggest, for example, that students at the top third of their class learn at a rate that is at least three times that of students in the bottom third (Gentile & Lalley, 2003). A well-designed video game is carefully crafted by developers to ensure that players are able to engage with the game, regardless of their prior gaming experience or skill. Developers can also design the games to adapt immediately to the individual differences of each player, allowing some to go faster or slower, and to change or skip goals as the player's skill and interest allow. This is much easier to do in a video game than in a classroom, where teachers frequently must teach the same curricula to the full class, without the ability to vary instructional pace for each student.

6.1.2 The Melding of Instruction, Practice, and Feedback

Video games, by design, require that content and procedural learning are typically coupled with practice. In contrast to stand-alone instruction, the immediate opportunity to engage with and use concepts *in vivo* immediately communicates the usefulness of a given concept. In addition, learners are provided with immediate feedback regarding their practice. Practice and feedback are interlaced during game play – players attempt a task, receive feedback, and practice again until they reach a point of mastery. Practicing to the point of mastery is predictive of both how much one remembers and of how quickly one can relearn something after initial forgetting. In contrast, traditional class instruction typically includes gaps of days or even weeks between the times when students receive instruction, practice the learned concepts and skills, and receive feedback after taking a test.

6.1.3 Overlearning and Sequenced Difficulty

Once skills or knowledge have been learned to the point of mastery, continued practice provides the opportunity for overlearning. Overlearning allows skills and knowledge to become solidified in memory and automatized, further allowing cognitive resources to be freed for learners to draw upon and apply new concepts and information. When students learn to read, for example, they must first sound out each letter until they can guess at the word. As this process is repeatedly practiced, the processing of words becomes automatized, and then the meanings of whole passages can come into focus (Bloom, 1986).

Most video games are designed with mastery and automaticity in mind. Early levels train basic game skills, such as how to move, jump, and shoot. Players can often spend as much time on these basic skills as they want, mastering and automatizing them. Later game levels are often impossible if the basic skills have not been automatized so that they can be combined or more complex skills can be learned and used. At the beginning of many games, for example, there are "training modes" in which players are slowly exposed to each of the controls used in the game, and players are often allowed to continue playing at a lower difficulty (e.g., replaying a level) until the necessary skills have been mastered. In a well-designed game, the difficulty and complexity of tasks are carefully sequenced so that players are not overwhelmed and give up. Instead, they are designed to allow for some challenge to help motivate repeated practice to the point that players master the necessary skills for future game success.

6.1.4 Motivation for Learning in the Face of Frustration

Video games are motivating in many ways. We may be interested by the story, characters, and graphics, but games also have motivating mechanisms of both intrinsic and extrinsic motivations. Players are rewarded with points, increased character levels, abilities, better weapons and gear, in-game currency, improvements in character status such as in health or ammo capacity, and access to new components of the story line. The timing of these gains are usually variable, which increases perseverance even in the face of frustration (although there may be some fixed-ratio reinforcements also to make sure that one doesn't go too long without some reinforcement).

Similarly, players are constantly reaching goals and earning access to new levels of complexity. This should promote self-efficacy and the self-esteem that results from competence. Theorists have stated that self-efficacy arises from competence (Bandura, 1977), and that lack of competence can lead to learned helplessness (Seligman, 1975). Thus, perceived competence can be an important motivator for continued practice.

In addition, intrinsic motivation is highly related to how well a given task fills the needs for autonomy, relatedness, and competence (Self-Determination Theory; e.g., Ryan & Deci, 2000). Games are excellent at filling all of these needs, which is highly motivating. Causing your game character to do specific things with the controller you are holding will give some sense of control (autonomy). As you play more, you will have an increasing sense of competence, which also should increase the sense of autonomy. Games also fill relatedness needs, both within games (such as when playing multiplayer games either in the same room or across the internet) and outside of the games themselves (such as talking with friends who also like the same game). In contrast, many classroom settings do a poor job meeting students' needs to feel in control, competent, or connected.

6.1.5 Optimized Massed and Distributed Practice

The motivational and feedback processes provide a learning environment in which learners, when encountering failure, often continue trying until they show progress. When a new game is purchased, gamers often put in a great deal of time right away, that is, massing their practice to begin to learn the basics. With each new skill needed in a game (e.g., new character abilities, weapons, game maps), players typically exercise this skill over many practice trials. As players continue to play, those same skills are periodically called upon, which distributes practice of that skill. The initial massed practice coupled with subsequent distributed practice is an outstanding model for learning. This process builds mastery with continual reinforcement of each skill, allowing learners to relearn what was forgotten, provide new cues for memory, interpret information in new contexts so that memories can be organized to promote generalization, build attitudes and beliefs that support learned content, and automatize relevant knowledge structures.

6.1.6 Generalization and Transfer

The gold standard of education is to teach for transfer, but this is very difficult to achieve in the classroom. Yet, video games (and mass media in general) seem to be able to achieve it almost effortlessly. For example, the effect of violent games on aggressive behavior is an example of far transfer, given that the way aggression is demonstrated in the real world usually looks nothing like what is practiced in games. How is this achieved?

Video games allow players to exercise skills, knowledge, and even attitudes in several different contexts under varying conditions with multiple methods. Transfer is most likely in this type of situation, where one practices and learns the deep underlying constants that can be applied to different specific situations (e.g., Perry, Samuelson, Malloy, & Schiffer, 2010). When practicing any given skill in a variety of contexts, learners are able to identify and abstract the most relevant features of a skill as it becomes increasingly clear that these features are useful across contexts (Bransford, Brown, & Cocking, 2000). Practice in varied contexts also allows learners to associate the learned concept with a variety of cues that would be unavailable if practice occurred in a single setting (Brown, Collins, & Duguid, 1989). As an example, gamers who play violent video games appear to transfer aggressive attitudes and behaviors to the real world more if they play a range of game contexts (e.g., police, war, science fiction, zombie). By playing in multiple contexts, the common theme (i.e., that violence is an acceptable, or preferred, approach to resolving conflicts) is made more salient and transfers more easily (Gentile & Gentile, 2008).

7 Using the GLM to Address Controversies

A theory is only as useful as its ability to organize empirical facts, make predictions, and resolve questions and controversies. A general learning theory should be no exception, and it is relevant to social psychology in that most social behaviors have a learned component. Let's examine how it might relate to a couple of the controversies in the literature on video games.

The greatest controversy has been over interpreting the research on violent video games, and on media violence in general (for a history of this controversy, see Gentile & Murray, 2014). The first major review was conducted by the US Surgeon General's scientific advisory committee, and it included a survey of the existing research as well as about 60 new federally-funded projects conducted by over 100 researchers, released in a report accompanied by 5 volumes of reports by the research teams (which can be accessed online at the National Library of Medicine, e.g., http://profiles.nlm.nih.gov/ps/access/NNBCGX.pdf). Controversy began immediately, as about half of the committee members had ties with the entertainment industry and the industry was allowed to veto the leading social psychologists, such as Albert Bandura and Leonard Berkowitz, from participating. Nonetheless, the report concluded that there was "fairly substantial" causal evidence. Sadly, the *New York Times* leaked a summary under the incorrect headline "TV Violence Held Unharmful to Youth," leading the public to believe the opposite of what the report actually said.

Several more major scientific reviews have been conducted, including by the National Institute of Mental Health (1982), the American Psychological Association (APA Committee on Violence in Video Games and Interactive Media, 2005; APA Task Force on Violent Media, 2015; Huston et al., 1992), the US Surgeon General (2001), the International Society for Research on Aggression (2012), the Society for the Psychological Study of Social Issues (Anderson, Bushman, Donnerstein, Hummer, & Warburton, 2014), the American Academy of Pediatrics (American Academy of Pediatrics Committee on Communications and Media, 2009; American Academy of Pediatrics Committee on Public Education, 2001; Anderson et al., 2017), the National Science Foundation (Subcommittee on Youth Violence, 2013), and the American Medical Association, among others (American Academy of Pediatrics, American Psychological Association, American Academy of Child

& Adolescent Psychiatry, & American Medical Association, 2000). As one can see, these are the major public health and scientific organizations that we rely on to vet the science. They agree that violent video games (and violent media in general) are one causal risk factor for aggression.

In addition, many meta-analyses have been conducted and they also find essentially the same effect size (e.g., Anderson, 2004; Anderson & Bushman, 2001, 2002a; Anderson et al., 2010; Bushman & Huesmann, 2006; Calvert et al., 2017; Comstock & Scharrer, 2003; Drummond, Sauer, & Ferguson, 2020; Ferguson, 2007a, 2007b; Greitemeyer & Mügge, 2014; Paik & Comstock, 1994; Savage & Yancey, 2008; Sherry, 2001). That is, they generally find a small effect of $r = .05$ to $.20$ between violent video games and aggression. Even most of the critics' meta-analyses find the same result, but they tend to interpret it as unimportant or dismiss it by claiming publication bias.

Examining one of the most cited of these critical meta-analyses, Ferguson (2007a) finds a significant effect of violent games on aggressive behaviors at $r = .29$. He provides some evidence of publication bias, and suggests a corrected effect size of $r = .15$. What is interesting is that he also finds significant effects of violent games on aggressive physiology and aggressive thoughts, which he does not dispute.

Despite the apparent scientific consensus, controversies about this body of research have increased, particularly when the research is discussed in the public domain – usually with reference to a school shooting or other tragedy. In this highly charged context, the argument has become more polarized and politicized, with the gun lobby blaming violent games, for example, whereas the gaming lobby points the finger at guns. The controversy has entered the scientific discussion too, with some camps claiming that the debate should be "over" (e.g., Anderson, Gentile, & Buckley, 2007; Committee on the Judiciary, 1994) and other camps claiming that violent games have no effects whatsoever and that researchers are trying to foment a "moral panic" (e.g., Ferguson, 2008; Markey & Ferguson, 2017b). Both of these positions are extreme and difficult to support.

Debates are never "over" as long as someone wants to debate. More importantly, however, science should always be open to new data, and theories need to adapt as new methods open up new findings.

With regard to the claim that violent games have no effects, these arguments rest primarily on some null results. Null results by themselves are not good evidence for the absence of an effect, especially when meta-analyses include these null-effect studies and continue to find significant effects overall. Many of these null results papers used inappropriately small sample sizes (given the estimate of the effect size at about $r = .15$, the minimum should be at least

100 per condition, and substantially more if interactions are sought; e.g., Devilly, Callahan, & Armitage, 2012; Kneer, Elson, & Knapp, 2016; Kühn et al., 2019). Others compare violent games with violent games, rather than neutral or prosocial games (e.g., Hilgard, Engelhardt, Rouder, Segert, & Bartholow, 2019; Kneer, Elson, & Knapp, 2016). More importantly, however, this argument makes little sense when one recognizes that this effect is, at its core, about learning. How could one practice with something for hours on end and *not* get better at it? We would need substantial theoretical justification to explain how learning is *prevented* from happening with video games.

Furthermore, even studies that show weak or null results on aggressive behavior still generally find that violent games can affect aggressive thoughts, feelings, and physiology. Figure 6 describes thoughts, feelings, and physiology as the present internal state, and these three can not only influence each other, but also behaviors. Again, the critics never offer theoretical justification how cognition and affect can be influenced without leaking out into behaviors.

To add to the confusion, not every area of gaming research has been met with equal resistance. This strikes us as funny, because the learning mechanisms underlying most effects are identical – therefore, if critics accept some of the effects (such as for educational games, prosocial games, serious games, and games for health), they should accept the others (e.g., violent games) because the psycho-logical learning mechanisms underlying the effects are essentially identical.

Nonetheless, there have been some similar controversies in other research domains, such as in response to the World Health Organization's inclusion of gaming disorder in the ICD-11. This was met with strong resistance by groups of researchers and activists claiming that there was no need to "pathologize" a normative behavior such as gaming (e.g., Bean, Nielsen, Van Rooij, & Ferguson, 2017), and the unsubstantiated claim of "moral panic" was once again raised (e.g., Markey & Ferguson, 2017a).

We are not clinicians, and leave the clinical aspects of this debate to other experts. Nonetheless, addictions have social, behavioral, and learned aspects to them. From a behavioral learning theory perspective, becoming "a slave to a habit" involves positive and negative reinforcement on a scheduling spiral that maintains, and likely exacerbates, the habit. Regarding schedules, the longer the at-risk individuals are deprived of a game (or a drug), the more they crave it. This craving manifests itself as an annoying feeling – an aversive stimulus – the escape from which is negatively reinforcing. That is, the individual escapes the anxiety of other feelings of being deprived of the game (or drug), and subse-quently is likely to repeat the game-playing (or drug-taking) behavior.

Once one escapes from the negative feelings, one also can enjoy the positive feelings associated with engaging in the behaviors (i.e., the fun, challenge, and rewards of the game). Combine these positive reinforcement effects with the negative (escape or avoidance) reinforcement effects, and learning theory predicts an increasing probability of gaining gaming disorder symptoms.

Well-designed games also include intermittent reinforcement in several ways. First, the challenges often have a random aspect, making them vary in how easy they are to overcome. Second, the reward for defeating a level or an enemy is often of variable value, with high value rewards occurring more rarely. Third, there is usually more than one way to solve a game problem or defeat an enemy, which adds uncertainty for the players to know how or when they will succeed. As noted previously, variable reinforcement is the best way to get people to continue a behavior, even in the face of frustration and punishment (see Section 3.6).

One additional point about schedule: By the time gamers are diagnosed with a disorder, they have become fairly skilled with their favorite games, usually resulting from a considerable amount of both massed and distributed practice. The latter also provides intermittent reinforcement, which increases the probability or strength of a habit.

In addition to these operant mechanics, several other learning processes are at play. To the extent that one repeats playing, various emotions and attitudes about gaming can become conditioned (such as one needs to play games to cope with difficult situations). If one identifies as a gamer, this will likely moderate other learning processes and beliefs.

There is more that could be said about how many of the attitudes, feelings, and behaviors underlie an addictive disorder, but the point we are making is that the GLM can help to examine the controversy over gaming disorder. Behaviors that are initially adaptive and functional can become obsessive and dysfunctional through basic learning processes and repeated practice. Therefore, the critics who claim (without any evidence we have ever seen) that researchers are attempting to generate a moral "panic" and pathologize normal behaviors do not seem to recognize that it is possible to create pathological behavior patterns through simple learning mechanisms.

7.1 Conclusions

We argue that many of the current controversies could be at least partly resolved with a learning theory perspective. We also believe that this is not limited to video game research, but to a great deal of social psychology. Many, maybe most, of the topics that social psychologists study have learning as a core aspect, including human aggression, prosocial behavior, prejudice, stereotypes, group norms, social identity, and so on. Thus, it is useful to have a clear description of how learning is active within social domains.

As the GLM shows, learning is not monolithic; it is dynamic and several psychological processes can moderate it. These include motivational/emotional states, stress, social context, sleep, interference from other learning sources, and practice schedules. Furthermore, each of the different learning mechanisms can support or interact with the others, and some appear necessarily dependent on others.

There has been a lot of interest in "gamifying" education, from elementary school through workplace training. Although we agree that games do an excellent job of motivating and training, we do not think they are such effective teachers because of the *game* elements, such as scores or badges. Instead, we think they are effective because they are carefully designed to teach through multiple learning mechanisms (e.g., variable reinforcement schedules, discrimination, and habituation learning) with a focus on the processes of learning (e.g., a well-structured spiral curriculum), and support for many of the moderators of learning (e.g., emotional involvement, early massed practice followed by distributed practice). The lesson to be learned is not simply that games teach because they are "fun," but because they go well beyond fun to use many of the best practices of teaching that are known from the past 130 years of psychological research. The GLM describes what learners have to do to (1) progress through the S-shaped learning curve, (2) relearn and overlearn to a high standard, and (3) recall material and skills in a number of contexts, so that the material and skills can transfer and thus be truly usable. This can be accomplished intentionally, such as gamifying education, or unintentionally, when games are played for entertainment. In either case, learning happens.

With this first comprehensive description of the GLM, we request that people put it to the test. Several areas appear to be ripe for exploration. These include where different learning mechanisms intersect, such as demonstrating that discrimination is necessary before association learning is possible (or not), under what conditions learning can happen from single exposures and how repeated exposure changes the types of learning that may occur, and how learning mechanisms interact to improve learning (or not). It will be a difficult theory to falsify because almost all of the pieces have been tested and refined for decades. It also will be difficult to be able to separate out which learning mechanisms are working for a given task and in what order. Nonetheless, these types of methodological challenges are what social psychologists excel at overcoming.

Most of the work that has cited the GLM to date has been in the video game domain. This is a quirk of how it developed out of research on prosocial video games, but the GLM is a general model for all of human learning in all domains. We would like to see it tested in multiple domains, especially outside of controversial areas where there may be biases both for and against it. Any null result study of, say, violent games and aggression will not be good evidence against the GLM, nor will any study finding an effect be strong evidence for it. These types of studies focus only on the broad strokes, and many other variables can affect whether significant relations are found (measures, cover story, inappropriate statistical controls, etc.; see Kim, Anderson, & Gentile, 2021, for more details). Good tests will examine the details of learning to see if they occur in the orders, combinations, and interactions that can be hypothesized from the GLM. There is not likely to be controversy with the broad idea that experience with something (especially repeated experience) generates learning. Thus, any studies that fail to show learning are much more likely to teach us something about when learning can be inhibited rather than to be a criticism of the GLM as a whole. These will be very fruitful areas to explore.

We have been impressed with the significant findings and theorizing by researchers over the past hundred years in these many domains of learning. No one approach seems dominant. Indeed, they all seem complementary, even synergistic, in allowing for a comprehensive view of learning. We are hopeful that this updated and expanded description of the GLM can help to generate novel scientific hypotheses, to guide the development of effective training methods, to provide insight into issues both theoretical and practical, and to resolve some of the current and future debates in social psychology.

References

Ahmad, F. (2006). British Muslim perceptions and opinions on news coverage of September 11. *Journal of Ethnic and Migration Studies, 32*(6), 961–982. http://doi.org/10.1080/13691830600761479.

American Academy of Pediatrics, American Psychological Association, American Academy of Child & Adolescent Psychiatry, & American Medical Association. (2000). Joint statement on the impact of entertainment violence on children. Retrieved from www.aap.org/advocacy/releases/jstmtevc.htm; www.aacap.org/press_releases/2000/0726.htm.

American Academy of Pediatrics Committee on Communications and Media. (2009). Media violence. *Pediatrics, 124*, 1495–1503.

American Academy of Pediatrics Committee on Public Education. (2001). Media violence. *Pediatrics, 108*, 1222–1225.

Amsel, A. (1962). Frustrative nonreward in partial reinforcement and discrimination learning: Some recent history and a theoretical extension. *Psychological Review, 69*(4), 306–328. http://doi.org/10.1037/h0046200.

Anderson, C. A. (2004). An update on the effects of playing violent video games. *Journal of Adolescence, 27*, 113–122.

Anderson, C. A., Berkowitz, L., Donnerstein, E., Huesmann, L. R., Johnson, J. D., Linz, D., ... Wartella, E. (2003). The influence of media violence on youth. *Psychological Science in the Public Interest, 4*, 81–110.

Anderson, C. A. & Bushman, B. J. (2001). Effects of violent video games on aggressive behavior, aggressive cognition, aggressive affect, physiological arousal, and prosocial behavior: A meta-analytic review of the scientific literature. *Psychological Science, 12*, 353–359.

Anderson, C. A. & Bushman, B. J. (2002a). The effects of media violence on society. *Science, 295*, 2377–2379.

Anderson, C. A. & Bushman, B. J. (2002b). The general aggression model: An integrated social-cognitive model of human aggression. *Annual Review of Psychology, 53*, 27–51.

Anderson, C. A. & Bushman, B. J. (2002c). Human aggression. *Annual Review of Psychology, 53*, 27–51.

Anderson, C. A., Bushman, B. J., Bartholow, B. D., Cantor, J., Christakis, D., Coyne, S. M., ... Ybarra, M. (2017). Screen violence and youth behavior. *Pediatrics, 140*(Supplement 2), S142–S147. http://doi.org/10.1542/peds.2016-1758t.

Anderson, C. A., Bushman, B. J., Donnerstein, E., Hummer, T. A., & Warburton, W. (2014). SPSSI research summary on media violence. Retrieved from www.spssi.org/index.cfm?fuseaction=page.viewPage &pageID=1899&nodeID=1.

Anderson, C. A., Carnagey, N. L., Flanagan, M., Benjamin, A. J. J., Eubanks, J., & Valentine, J. C. (2004). Violent video games: Specific effects of violent content on aggressive thoughts and behavior. *Advances in Experimental Social Psychology, 36,* 199–249.

Anderson, C. A., Deuser, W. E., & DeNeve, K. M. (1995). Hot temperatures, hostile affect, hostile cognition, and arousal: Tests of a general model of affective aggression. *Personality and Social Psychology Bulletin, 21*(5), 434–448.

Anderson, C. A. & Dill, K. (2000). Video games and aggressive thoughts, feelings, and behavior in the laboratory and in life. *Journal of Personality and Social Psychology, 78*(4), 772–790. http://doi.org/10.1037/0022-3514 .78.4.772.

Anderson, C. A., Gentile, D. A., & Buckley, K. E. (2007). *Violent video game effects on children and adolescents: Theory, research, and public policy.* New York: Oxford University Press.

Anderson, C. A., Gentile, D. A., & Dill, K. E. (2012). Prosocial, antisocial, and other effects of recreational video games. In D. G. Singer & J. L. Singer (eds.), *Handbook of children and the media* (2nd ed., pp. 249–272). Thousand Oaks, CA: Sage.

Anderson, C. A., Shibuya, A., Ihori, N., Swing, E. L., Bushman, B. J., Sakamoto, A., . . . Saleem, M. (2010). Violent video game effects on aggression, empathy, and prosocial behavior in eastern and western countries: A meta-analytic review. *Psychological Bulletin, 136*(2), 151–173. http://doi.org /10.1037/a0018251.

Anderson, J. R. (1982). Acquisition of cognitive skill. *Psychological Review, 89* (4), 369.

APA Committee on Violence in Video Games and Interactive Media. (2005). APA calls for reduction of violence in interactive media used by children and adolescents. Retrieved from www.craiganderson.org/wp-content/uploads/ caa/VGVpolicyDocs/05APA.pdf.

APA Task Force on Violent Media. (2015). *Technical report on the review of the violent video game literature.* Washington, DC: American Psychological Association.

Ash, E. (2016). Priming or Proteus effect? Examining the effects of avatar race on in-game behavior and post-play aggressive cognition and affect in video games. *Games and Culture, 11*(4), 422–440. http://doi.org/10.1177 /1555412014568870.

Aslin, R. N. & Newport, E. L. (2012). Statistical learning: From acquiring specific items to forming general rules. *Current Directions in Psychological Science, 21*(3), 170–176.

Baehre, M. R. & Gentile, J. R. (1991). Cumulative effects of the keyword mnemonic and distributed practice in learning social studies facts: A classroom evaluation. *Journal of Research in Education, 1*(1), 70–78.

Bahrick, H. P. (1984). Semantic memory content in permastore: Fifty years of memory for Spanish learned in school. *Journal of Experimental Psychology: General, 113*(1), 1.

Bailey, K., West, R., & Anderson, C. A. (2010). A negative association between video game experience and proactive cognitive control. *Psychophysiology, 47*, 34–42. http://doi.org/10.1111/j.1469-8986.2009.00925.x.

Bandura, A. (1965). Influence of models' reinforcement contingencies on the acquisition of imitative responses. *Journal of Personality and Social Psychology, 1*(6), 589–595.

Bandura, A. (1977). *Social learning theory.* Englewood Cliffs, NJ: Prentice Hall.

Bandura, A. (1986). *Social foundations of thought and action: A social cognitive theory.* Englewood Cliffs, NJ: Prentice-Hall.

Bandura, A. & Kupers, C. J. (1964). Transmission of patterns of self-reinforcement through modeling. *The Journal of Abnormal and Social Psychology, 69*(1), 1–9. http://doi.org/10.1037/h0041187.

Bandura, A., Ross, D., & Ross, S. A. (1963). Imitation of film-mediated aggressive models. *Journal of Abnormal and Social Psychology, 66*, 3–11.

Bartlett, F. C. (1932). *Remembering: A study in experimental and social psychology.* Cambridge: Cambridge University Press.

Barlett, N. D., Gentile, D. A., Barlett, C. P., Eisenmann, J. C., & Walsh, D. A. (2012). Sleep as a mediator of screen time effects on American children's health outcomes: A prospective study. *Journal of Children and Media, 6*, 37–50.

Barnett, S. M. & Ceci, S. J. (2002). When and where do we apply what we learn? A taxonomy for far transfer. *Psychological Bulletin, 128*(4), 612.

Bean, A. M., Nielsen, R. K., Van Rooij, A. J., & Ferguson, C. J. (2017). Video game addiction: The push to pathologize video games. *Professional Psychology: Research and Practice, 48*(5), 378.

Bègue, L., Sarda, E., Gentile, D. A., Bry, C., & Roché, S. (2017). Video games exposure and sexism in a representative sample of adolescents. *Frontiers in Psychology, 8*, 466. http://doi.org/10.3389/fpsyg.2017.00466.

Behm-Morawitz, E. & Ta, D. (2014). Cultivating virtual stereotypes? The impact of video game play on racial/ethnic stereotypes. *Howard Journal*

of Communications, 25(1), 1–15. http://doi.org/10.1080/10646175.2013
.835600.

Bender, P. K. & Gentile, D. A. (2020). Internet gaming disorder: Relations
between needs satisfaction in-game and in life in general. *Psychology of
Popular Media, 9*(2), 266–278. http://doi.org/10.1037/ppm0000227.

Bloom, B. S. (1986). Automaticity: "The hands and feet of genius."
Educational Leadership, 43(5), 70–77.

Bloom, K. C. & Shuell, T. J. (1981). Effects of massed and distributed practice
on the learning and retention of second-language vocabulary. *The Journal of
Educational Research, 74*(4), 245–248.

Böhm, T., Ruth, N., & Schramm, H. (2016). "Count on me" – the influence of
music with prosocial lyrics on cognitive and affective aggression.
Psychomusicology: Music, Mind, and Brain, 26(3), 279–283. http://doi.org
/10.1037/pmu0000155.

Boot, W., Blakely, D., & Simons, D. (2011). Do action video games improve
perception and cognition? *Frontiers in Psychology, 2*, 226. Retrieved from
www.frontiersin.org/article/10.3389/fpsyg.2011.00226.

Boulton, M. J. (2012). Children's hostile attribution bias is reduced after
watching realistic playful fighting, and the effect is mediated by prosocial
thoughts. *Journal of Experimental Child Psychology, 113*(1), 36–48. http://
doi.org/10.1016/j.jecp.2012.02.011.

Bowen, E., Walker, K., Mawer, M., Holdsworth, E., Sorbring, E.,
Helsing, B., ... Jans, S. (2014). "It's like you're actually playing as
yourself": Development and preliminary evaluation of "Green Acres
High," a serious game-based primary intervention to combat adolescent
dating violence+. *Psychosocial Intervention, 23*(1), 43–55. http://doi.org
/10.5093/in2014a5.

Bower, G. H. & Hilgard, E. R. (1981). *Theories of learning*: Englewood Cliffs,
NJ: Prentice-Hall.

Bransford, J. D., Brown, A. L., & Cocking, R. R. (2000). *How people learn*
(Vol. 11). Washington, DC: National Academy Press.

Bregman, E. O. (1934). An attempt to modify the emotional attitudes of infants
by the conditioned response technique. *The Pedagogical Seminary and
Journal of Genetic Psychology, 45*, 169–198. http://doi.org/10.1080
/08856559.1934.10534254.

Bridger, W. H. (1961). Sensory habituation and discrimination in the human
neonate. *American Journal of Psychiatry, 117*(11), 991–996. http://doi.org/10
.1176/ajp.117.11.991.

Brown, J. S., Collins, A., & Duguid, P. (1989). Situated cognition and the
culture of learning. *Educational Researcher, 18*(1), 32–42.

Brown, R. & Kulik, J. (1977). Flashbulb memories. *Cognition*, 5(1), 73–99.

Bruer, J. T. (1997). Education and the brain: A bridge too far. *Educational Researcher*, 26(8), 4–16. http://doi.org/10.3102/0013189x026008004.

Buckley, K. E. & Anderson, C. A. (2006). A theoretical model of the effects and consequences of playing video games. In P. Vorderer & J. Bryant (eds.), *Playing video games – Motives, responses, and consequences* (pp. 363–378). Mahwah, NJ: LEA.

Bugelski, B. R. (1979). *Principles of learning and memory*. New York: Praeger.

Burgess, M. C. R., Dill, K. E., Stermer, S. P., Burgess, S. R., & Brown, B. P. (2011). Playing with prejudice: The prevalence and consequences of racial stereotypes in video games. *Media Psychology*, 14(3), 289–311. http://doi .org/10.1080/15213269.2011.596467.

Busching, R. & Krahé, B. (2013). Charging neutral cues with aggressive meaning through violent video game play. *Societies*, 3(4), 445–456. http://doi .org/10.3390/soc3040445.

Bushman, B. J. & Huesmann, L. R. (2006). Short-term and long-term effects of violent media on aggression in children and adults. *Archives of Pediatrics & Adolescent Medicine*, 160(4), 348–352. Retrieved from http://archpedi.ama-assn.org/cgi/content/abstract/160/4/348.

Cahill, L., Haier, R. J., Fallon, J., Alkire, M. T., Tang, C., Keator, D., … McGaugh, J. L. (1996). Amygdala activity at encoding correlated with long-term, free recall of emotional information. *Proceedings of the National Academy of Sciences*, 93(15), 8016–8021. http://doi.org/10.1073 /pnas.93.15.8016.

Cain, L. F. & Willey, R. D. V. (1939). The effect of spaced learning on the curve of retention. *Journal of Experimental Psychology*, 25(2), 209.

Cairney, S. A., Durrant, S. J., Musgrove, H., & Lewis, P. A. (2011). Sleep and environmental context: Interactive effects for memory. *Experimental Brain Research*, 214(1), 83.

Calvert, S. L., Appelbaum, M., Dodge, K. A., Graham, S., Nagayama Hall, G. C., Hamby, S., … Hedges, L. V. (2017). The American Psychological Association Task Force assessment of violent video games: Science in the service of public interest. *American Psychologist*, 72(2), 126–143. http://doi.org/10.1037/a0040413.

Carpenter, S. K. (2017). Spacing effects on learning and memory. In J. H. Byrne (ed.), *Learning and memory: A comprehensive reference* (Vol. 2, pp. 465–485). Oxford, UK: Academic Press.

Carpenter, S. K. & Geller, J. (2020). Is a picture really worth a thousand words? Evaluating contributions of fluency and analytic processing in metacognitive judgements for pictures in foreign language vocabulary learning. *Quarterly Journal of Experimental Psychology, 73*(2), 211–224.

Carpenter, S. K., Witherby, A. E., & Tauber, S. K. (2020). On students' (mis) judgments of learning and teaching effectiveness: Where we stand and how to move forward. *Journal of Applied Research in Memory and Cognition, 9* (2), 181–185. http://doi.org/10.1016/J.JARMAC.2020.04.003.

Ceci, S. J., DeSimone Leichtman, M., Putnick, M., & Nightingale, N. N. (1993). The suggestibility of children's recollections. In D. Cicchetti & S. Toth (eds.), *Child abuse, child development, and social policy* (pp. 117–137). Norwood, NJ: Ablex.

Chall, J. S. & Jacobs, V. A. (2003). The classic study on poor children's fourth-grade slump. *American Educator, 27*(1), 14–15.

Challis, B. H., Velichkovsky, B. M., & Craik, F. I. M. (1996). Levels-of-processing effects on a variety of memory tasks: New findings and theoretical implications. *Consciousness and Cognition, 5*(1–2), 142–164. http://doi.org /10.1006/ccog.1996.0009.

Chang, J. H. & Bushman, B. J. (2019). Effect of exposure to gun violence in video games on children's dangerous behavior with real guns. *JAMA Network Open, 2*(5), e194319. http://doi.org/10.1001/jamanetworkopen.2019.4319.

Charness, N. (1976). Memory for chess positions: Resistance to interference. *Journal of Experimental Psychology: Human Learning and Memory, 2*(6), 641.

Chase, W. G. & Ericsson, K. A. (1981). Skilled memory. In John R. Anderson (ed.), *Cognitive skills and their acquisition* (pp. 141–189). Hillsdale, NJ: Erlbaum.

Chase, W. G. & Simon, H. A. (1973). Perception in chess. *Cognitive Psychology, 4*(1), 55–81.

Colombo, J. & Mitchell, D. W. (2009). Infant visual habituation. *Neurobiology of Learning and Memory, 92*(2), 225–234. http://doi.org/10.1016/j .nlm.2008.06.002.

Committee on the Judiciary. (1994). *Implementation of the Television Program Improvement Act of 1990: Joint Hearings Before the Subcommittee on the Constitution and the Subcommittee on Juvenile Justice of the Committee on the Judiciary, United States Senate, One Hundred Third Congress, First Session ... May 21 and June 8, 1993.* (J-103–13). Washington, DC: U.S. Government Printing Office.

Comstock, G. & Scharrer, E. (2003). Meta-analyzing the controversy over television violence and aggression. In D. A. Gentile (ed.), *Media violence and children: A complete guide for parents and professionals* (pp. 205–226). Westport, CT: Praeger.

Comstock, G. A. & Rubenstein, E. A. (1972). Television and social behavior; Reports and Papers, Volume III. Television and Adolescent Aggressiveness. https://www.ojp.gov/ncjrs/virtual-library/abstracts/television-and-social-behavior-reports-and-papers-volume-iii.

Coyne, S. M., Stockdale, L. A., Warburton, W., Gentile, D. A., Yang, C., & Merrill, B. M. (2020). Pathological video game symptoms from adolescence to emerging adulthood: A 6-year longitudinal study of trajectories, predictors, and outcomes. *Developmental Psychology, Advance Online Publication, 56*(7), 1385–1396. http://doi.org/10.1037/dev0000939.

Craik, F. I. & Tulving, E. (1975). Depth of processing and the retention of words in episodic memory. *Journal of Experimental Psychology: General, 104*(3), 268.

Cutrell, E., Czerwinski, M., & Horvitz, E. (2001). *Notification, disruption, and memory: Effects of messaging interruptions on memory and performance.* Paper presented at the Human-Computer Interaction – INTERACT'01, Tokyo.

Decker, J. H., Otto, A. R., Daw, N. D., & Hartley, C. A. (2016). From creatures of habit to goal-directed learners: Tracking the developmental emergence of model-based reinforcement learning. *Psychological Science, 27*(6), 848–858.

DeGroot, A. D. (1965). Thought and mind in chess. *The Hague: Mouton* (1).

Devilly, G. J., Callahan, P., & Armitage, G. (2012). The effect of violent videogame playtime on anger. *Australian Psychologist, 47*(2), 98–107. http://doi.org/10.1111/j.1742-9544.2010.00008.x.

Dill, K. E., Gentile, D. A., Richter, W. A., & Dill, J. C. (2005). Violence, sex, race, and age in popular video games: A content analysis. In E. Cole & J. H. Daniel (eds.), *Featuring females: Feminist analyses of media* (pp. 115–130). Washington, DC: American Psychological Association.

Donnerstein, E., Slaby, R. G., & Eron, L. D. (1994). *The mass media and youth aggression.* Washington, DC: American Psychological Association.

Downs, E. & Smith, S. L. (2010). Keeping abreast of hypersexuality: A video game character content analysis. *Sex Roles, 62*(11–12), 721–733. http://doi.org/10.1007/s11199-009-9637-1.

Drummond, A., Sauer, J. D., & Ferguson, C. J. (2020). Do longitudinal studies support long-term relationships between aggressive game play and youth aggressive behaviour? A meta-analytic examination. *Royal Society Open Science, 7.* http://doi.org/10.1098/rsos.200373.

Dudai, Y. (2004). *Memory from A to Z: Keywords, concepts, and beyond.* Oxford, UK: Oxford University Press.

Dweck, C. S. (1986). Motivational processes affecting learning. *American Psychologist, 41*(10), 1040–1048. http://doi.org/10.1037/0003-066X.41.10.1040.

Dweck, C. S. & Licht, B. G. (1980). Learned helplessness and intellectual achievement. *Human Helplessness: Theory and Applications*, 197–221.

Dye, M. W. G., Green, C. S., & Bavelier, D. (2009). Increasing speed of processing with action video games. *Current Directions in Psychological Science, 18*, 321–326.

Eastin, M. S., Appiah, O., & Cicchirllo, V. (2009). Identification and the influence of cultural Stereotyping on postvideogame play hostility. *Human Communication Research, 35*(3), 337–356. http://doi.org/10.1111/j.1468 -2958.2009.01354.x.

Ebbinghaus, H. (1885/1964). *Memory: A contribution to experimental psychology*. Oxford: Dover.

Eichenbaum, H. (2008). *Learning & memory*. New York: WW Norton.

Ellis, H. & Hunt, R. (1993). Fundamentals of cognitive psychology. Madison (5th ed.). Dubuque, IA: Brown & Benchmark.

Entertainment Software Association. (January 13, 2011). *Flawed video game study to be released next week: Study produced by author with long anti-video game history*. Retrieved from Washington, DC.

Ericsson, K. A., Chase, W. G., & Faloon, S. (1980). Acquisition of a memory skill. *Science, 208*(4448), 1181–1182.

Fam, J. Y. (2018). Prevalence of internet gaming disorder in adolescents: A meta-analysis across three decades. *Scandinavian Journal of Psychology, 59* (5), 524–531. http://doi.org/10.1111/sjop.12459.

Ferguson, C. J. (2007a). Evidence for publication bias in video game violence effects literature. *Aggression and Violent Behavior, 12*, 1–33.

Ferguson, C. J. (2007b). The good, the bad and the ugly: A meta-analytic review of positive and negative effects of violent video games. *Psychiatric Quarterly, 78*, 309–316.

Ferguson, C. J. (2008). The school shooting/violent video game link: Causal relationship or moral panic? *Journal of Investigative Psychology and Offender Profiling, 5*(1–2), 25–37. http://doi.org/10.1002/jip.76.

Ferguson, C. J. & Beresin, E. (2017). Social science's curious war with pop culture and how it was lost: The media violence debate and the risks it holds for social science. *Preventive Medicine, 99*, 69–76. http://doi.org/10.1016/ j.ypmed.2017.02.009.

Ferguson, C. J., Brown, J. M., & Torres, A. V. (2018). Education or indoctrination? The accuracy of introductory psychology textbooks in covering controversial topics and urban legends about psychology. *Current Psychology, 37*(3), 574–582.

Ferster, C. B. & Skinner, B. F. (1957). *Schedules of reinforcement*. East Norwalk, CT: Appleton-Century-Crofts.

Fischer, P., Greitemeyer, T., Kastenmüller, A., Vogrincic, C., & Sauer, A. (2011). The effects of risk-glorifying media exposure on risk-positive cognitions, emotions, and behaviors: A meta-analytic review. *Psychological Bulletin, 137*(3), 367–390. http://doi.org/10.1037/a0022267.

Fiske, S. T., Cuddy, A. J., Glick, P., & Xu, J. (2002). A model of (often mixed) stereotype content: Competence and warmth respectively follow from perceived status and competition. *Journal of Personality and Social Psychology, 82*(6), 878.

Fiske, S. T. & Taylor, S. E. (1991). *Social cognition.* New York: McGraw-Hill.

Flavell, J. H. (1971). Stage-related properties of cognitive development. *Cognitive Psychology, 2*, 421–453.

Flavell, J. H. (1979). Metacognition and cognitive monitoring: A new area of cognitive–developmental inquiry. *American Psychologist, 34*(10), 906.

Flavell, J. H., Friedrichs, A. G., & Hoyt, J. D. (1970). Developmental changes in memorization processes. *Cognitive Psychology, 1*(4), 324–340.

Fontana, L. & Beckerman, A. (2004). Childhood violence prevention education using video games. *Information Technology in Childhood Education Annual, 2004* (1), 49–62.

Fox, J., Ralston, R. A., Cooper, C. K., & Jones, K. A. (2015). Sexualized avatars lead to women's self-objectification and acceptance of rape myths. *Psychology of Women Quarterly, 39*(3), 349–362. http://doi.org/10.1177 /0361684314553578.

Franceschini, S., Gori, S., Ruffino, M., Viola, S., Molteni, M., & Facoetti, A. (2013). Action video games make dyslexic children read better. *Current Biology, 23*(6), 462–466. http://doi.org/10.1016/j.cub.2013.01.044.

Garcia, J. & Ervin, F. (1968). Gustatory-visceral and telereceptor-cutaneous conditioning: Adaptation in internal and external milieus. *Communications in Behavioral Biology, 1*(Part A), 389–415.

Geen, R. G. (2001). *Human aggression* (2nd ed.). Buckingham: Open University Press.

Geller, J., Toftness, A. R., Armstrong, P. I., Carpenter, S. K., Manz, C. L., Coffman, C. R., & Lamm, M. H. (2018). Study strategies and beliefs about learning as a function of academic achievement and achievement goals. *Memory, 26*(5), 683–690.

Gentile, D. A. (2009). Pathological video game use among youth 8 to 18: A national study. *Psychological Science, 20*, 594–602.

Gentile, D. A. (2011). The multiple dimensions of video game effects. *Child Development Perspectives, 5*, 75–81.

Gentile, D. A. (2014). *Media violence and children: A complete guide for parents and professionals* (2nd ed.). Santa Barbara, CA: Praeger.

Gentile, D. A. & Anderson, C. A. (2003). Violent video games: The newest media violence hazard. In D. A. Gentile (ed.), *Media violence and children: A complete guide for parents and professionals* (pp. 131–152). Westport, CT: Praeger.

Gentile, D. A., Anderson, C. A., Yukawa, S., Saleem, M., Lim, K. M., Shibuya, A., . . . Sakamoto, A. (2009). The effects of prosocial video games on prosocial behaviors: International evidence from correlational, longitudinal, and experimental studies. *Personality and Social Psychology Bulletin*, *35*, 752–763.

Gentile, D. A., Bailey, K., Bavelier, D., Brockmyer, J. F., Cash, H., Coyne, S. M., . . . Young, K. (2017). Internet gaming disorder in children and adolescents. *Pediatrics*, *140*(Supplement 2), S81–S85. http://doi.org/10.1542/peds.2016-1758h.

Gentile, D. A. & Bushman, B. J. (2012). Reassessing media violence effects using a risk and resilience approach to understanding aggression. *Psychology of Popular Media Culture*, *1*, 138–151.

Gentile, D. A., Choo, H., Liau, A. K., Sim, T., Li, D., Fung, D., & Khoo, A. (2011). Pathological video game use among youths: A two-year longitudinal study. *Pediatrics*, *127*, e319–e329.

Gentile, D. A. & Gentile, J. R. (2008). Violent video games as exemplary teachers: A conceptual analysis. *Journal of Youth and Adolescence*, *9*, 127–141.

Gentile, D. A., Groves, C., & Gentile, J. R. (2014). The general learning model: Unveiling the learning potential from video games. In F. C. Blumberg (ed.), *Learning by playing: Video gaming in education* (pp. 121–142). New York: Oxford University Press.

Gentile, D. A., Li, D., Khoo, A., Prot, S., & Anderson, C. A. (2014). Mediators and moderators of long-term effects of violent video games on aggressive behavior: Practice, thinking, and action. *JAMA Pediatrics*, *168*(5), 450–457. http://doi.org/10.1001/jamapediatrics.2014.63.

Gentile, D. A., Lynch, P. J., Linder, J. R., & Walsh, D. A. (2004). The effects of violent video game habits on adolescent hostility, aggressive behaviors, and school performance. *Journal of Adolescence*, *27*(1), 5–22.

Gentile, D. A., Maier, J. A., Hasson, M. R., & de Bonetti, B. L. (2011). Parents' evaluation of media ratings a decade after the television ratings were introduced. *Pediatrics*, *128*, 36–44.

Gentile, D. A. & Murray, J. P. (2014). Media violence and public policy: Where we have been and where we should go next. In D. A. Gentile (ed.), *Media violence and children* (2nd ed., pp. 413–432). Santa Barbara, CA: ABC-Clio.

Gentile, D. A. & Sesma, A. (2003). Developmental approaches to understanding media effects on individuals. In D. A. Gentile (ed.), *Media violence and children: A complete guide for parents and professionals* (pp. 19–38). Westport, CT: Praeger.

Gentile, D. A., Swing, E. L., Lim, C. G., & Khoo, A. (2012). Video game playing, attention problems, and impulsiveness: Evidence of bi-directional causality. *Psychology of Popular Media Culture, 1*, 62–70.

Gentile, J. R. (2000). Transfer of learning. In Alan E. Kazdin, *Encyclopedia of psychology* (Vol. 5, pp. 13–16). Washington, DC: American Psychological Association/Oxford University Press.

Gentile, J. R. & Lalley, J. P. (2003). *Standards and mastery learning: Aligning teaching and assessment so all children can learn.* Thousand Oaks, CA: Corwin Press.

Gentile, J. R., Monaco, N., Iheozor-Ejiofor, I. E., Ndu, A. N., & Ogbonaya, P. K. (1982). Retention by "fast" and "slow" learners. *Intelligence, 6*(2), 125–138. http://doi.org/10.1016/0160-2896(82)90010-1.

Gentile, J. R. & Monaco, N. M. (1988). A learned helplessness analysis of perceived failure in mathematics. *Focus on Learning Problems in Mathematics, 10*(1), 15–28.

Gibson, E. J. (1963). Perceptual learning. *Annual Review of Psychology, 14*(1), 29–56. http://doi.org/10.1146/annurev.ps.14.020163.000333.

Gibson, E. J. (1969). *Principles of perceptual learning and development.* New York: Appleton-Century-Crofts.

Gibson, E. J. & Pick, A. D. (2000). *An ecological approach to perceptual learning and development.* Oxford: Oxford University Press.

Gibson, J. J. (1979). *The ecological approach to visual perception.* Boston, MA: Houghton Mifflin.

Godden, D. R. & Baddeley, A. D. (1975). Context-dependent memory in two natural environments: On land and underwater. *British Journal of Psychology, 66*, 325–331.

Gopher, D., Weil, M., & Bareket, T. (1994). Transfer of skill from a computer game trainer to flight. *Human Factors, 36*, 387–405.

Green, C. S. & Bavelier, D. (2003). Action video game modifies visual selective attention. *Nature, 423*, 534–537.

Green, C. S. & Bavelier, D. (2006). Enumeration versus multiple object tracking: The case of action video game players. *Cognition, 101*(1), 217–245. http://doi.org/10.1016/j.cognition.2005.10.004.

Green, C. S. & Bavelier, D. (2007). Action-video-game experience alters the spatial resolution of vision. *Psychological Science, 18*(1), 88–94. http://doi.org/10.1111/j.1467-9280.2007.01853.x.

Green, C. S., Li, R., & Bavelier, D. (2010). Perceptual learning during action video game playing. *Topics in Cognitive Science, 2*(2), 202–216. http://doi.org/10.1111/j.1756-8765.2009.01054.x.

Gregory, S. C. & Bunch, M. E. (1959). The relative retentive abilities of fast and slow learners. *The Journal of General Psychology, 60*(2), 173–181.

Greitemeyer, T., Agthe, M., Turner, R., & Gschwendtner, C. (2012). Acting prosocially reduces retaliation: Effects of prosocial video games on aggressive behavior. *European Journal of Social Psychology, 42*(2), 235–242. http://doi.org/10.1002/ejsp.1837.

Greitemeyer, T. & Mügge, D. O. (2014). Video games do affect social outcomes: A meta-analytic review of the effects of violent and prosocial video game play. *Personality & Social Psychology Bulletin, 40*, 578–589.

Greitemeyer, T. & Osswald, S. (2009). Prosocial video games reduce aggressive cognitions. *Journal of Experimental Social Psychology, 45*(4), 896–900. http://doi.org/10.1016/j.jesp.2009.04.005.

Greitemeyer, T., & Osswald, S. (2010). Effects of prosocial video games on prosocial behavior. *Journal of Personality and Social Psychology, 98*(2), 211–221. doi:10.1037/a0016997

Greitemeyer, T. & Osswald, S. (2011). Playing prosocial video games increases the accessibility of prosocial thoughts. *The Journal of Social Psychology, 151* (2), 121–128. http://doi.org/10.1080/00224540903365588.

Greitemeyer, T., Osswald, S., & Brauer, M. (2010). Playing prosocial video games increases empathy and decreases schadenfreude. *Emotion, 10*(6), 796.

Griffiths, M. D. (2000). Does internet and computer "addiction" exist? Some case study evidence. *CyberPsychology & Behavior, 3*, 211–218.

Grubb, J. (2020). NPD: The 20 best-selling games of 2019 in the U.S. Retrieved from https://venturebeat.com/2020/01/16/20-best-selling-games-of-2019/.

Guéguen, N., Jacob, C., & Lamy, L. (2010). "Love is in the air": Effects of songs with romantic lyrics on compliance with a courtship request. *Psychology of Music, 38*(3), 303–307. http://doi.org/10.1177/0305735609360428.

Hall, D. (Producer) (June 25, 2020). The Eliza effect. Retrieved from https://99percentinvisible.org/episode/the-eliza-effect/.

Halpern, A. R. & Bower, G. H. (1982). Musical expertise and melodic structure in memory for musical notation. *The American Journal of Psychology, 95*, 31–50.

Hebb, D. O. (1949). *The organization of behavior: A neuropsychological theory*. New York: Taylor & Francis.

Hebb, D. O. (1959). A neuropsychological theory. In S. E. Koch (ed.), *Psychology: A study of a science* (Vol. 1, pp. 622–643). New York: McGraw-Hill.

Hilgard, J., Engelhardt, C. R., Rouder, J. N., Segert, I. L., & Bartholow, B. D. (2019). Null effects of game violence, game difficulty, and 2D:4D digit ratio on aggressive behavior. *Psychological Science, 30*(4), 606–616. http://doi .org/10.1177/0956797619829688.

Huesmann, L. R. & Eron, L. D. (1986). *Television and the aggressive child: A cross-national comparison.* Hillsdale, NJ: Lawrence Erlbaum Associates.

Huesmann, L. R. & Guerra, N. G. (1997). Normative beliefs and the development of aggressive behavior. *Journal of Personality and Social Psychology, 72,* 1–12.

Hulse, S. H., Egeth, H., & Deese, J. (1980). *The psychology of learning.* New York: McGraw-Hill.

Hunter, I. (1978). *The role of memory in expert mental calculations.* London: Academic Press.

Huston, A. C., Donnerstein, E., Fairchild, H., Feshbach, N. D., Katz, P. A., Murray, J. P., . . . Zuckerman, D. M. (1992). *Big world, small screen: The role of television in American society.* Lincoln, NE: University of Nebraska Press.

International Society for Research on Aggression. (2012). Report of the media violence commission. *Aggressive Behavior, 38*(5), 335–341. http://doi.org /10.1002/ab.21443.

James, W. (1906). *Talks to teachers on psychology: And to students on some of live's ideals.* New York: Henry Holt.

Jin, Y. & Li, J. (2017). When newbies and veterans play together: The effect of video game content, context and experience on cooperation. *Computers in Human Behavior, 68,* 556–563. http://doi.org/10.1016/j.chb.2016.11.059.

Judd, C. H. (1908). The relation of special training and general intelligence. *Educational Review, 36,* 28–42.

Kahneman, D. (2011). *Thinking, fast and slow.* New York: Macmillan.

Keeney, T. J., Cannizzo, S. R., & Flavell, J. H. (1967). Spontaneous and induced verbal rehearsal in a recall task. *Child Development, 38,* 953–966.

Kim, E., Anderson, C. A., & Gentile, D. A. (2021). The 7 +/- 2 deadly sins of video game violence research. In V. C. Strasburger (ed.), *Masters of media* (Vol. 1, pp. 19–42). Lanham, MD: Rowman & Littlefield.

Kirsh, S. J. (1998). Seeing the world through Mortal Kombat-colored glasses: Violent video games and the development of a short-term hostile attribution bias. *Childhood, 5,* 177–184.

Kleinsmith, L. J. & Kaplan, S. (1963). Paired-associate learning as a function of arousal and interpolated interval. *Journal of Experimental Psychology, 65*(2), 190.

Kneer, J., Elson, M., & Knapp, F. (2016). Fight fire with rainbows: The effects of displayed violence, difficulty, and performance in digital games on affect, aggression, and physiological arousal. *Computers in Human Behavior, 54*, 142–148. http://doi.org/10.1016/j.chb.2015.07.034.

Konijn, E. A., Bijvank, M. N., & Bushman, B. J. (2007). I wish I were a warrior: The role of wishful identification in the effects of violent video games on aggression in adolescent boys. *Developmental Psychology, 43*(4), 1038–1044. http://doi.org/2007-09251-019 [pii] 10.1037/0012–1649.43.4.1038.

Krueger, W. C. F. (1929). The effect of overlearning on retention. *Journal of Experimental Psychology, 12*(1), 71–78. http://doi.org/10.1037/h0072036.

Kühn, S., Kugler, D. T., Schmalen, K., Weichenberger, M., Witt, C., & Gallinat, J. (2019). Does playing violent video games cause aggression? A longitudinal intervention study. *Molecular Psychiatry, 24*(8), 1220–1234. http://doi.org/10.1038/s41380-018-0031-7.

Langille, J. J. & Brown, R. E. (2018). The synaptic theory of memory: A historical survey and reconciliation of recent opposition. *Frontiers in Systems Neuroscience, 12*, 52–52. http://doi.org/10.3389/fnsys.2018.00052.

Lapierre, M. A. & Farrar, K. M. (2018). Learning to love guns? Gun-based gameplay's links to gun attitudes. *Psychology of Popular Media Culture, 7* (3), 216–230. http://doi.org/10.1037/ppm0000132.

Lazarus, R. S. (1982). Thoughts on the relations between emotion and cognition. *American Psychologist, 37*(9), 1019.

Lazarus, R. S. (1984). On the primacy of cognition. *American Psychologist, 39* (2), 124–129. http://doi.org/10.1037/0003-066X.39.2.124.

Li, J.-Y. & Jin, Y.-C. (2014). The effects of violent video games and prosocial video games on cognition, emotion and behavior. *Chinese Journal of Clinical Psychology, 22*(6), 985–988.

Li, R., Polat, U., Makous, W., & Bavelier, D. (2009). Enhancing the contrast sensitivity function through action video game training. *Nature Neuroscience, 12*, 549–551.

Li, R. W., Ngo, C., Nguyen, J., & Levi, D. M. (2011). Video-game play induces plasticity in the visual system of adults with amblyopia. *PLoS Biology, 9*(8), e1001135. http://doi.org/10.1371/journal.pbio.1001135.

Libet, B., Gleason, C. A., Wright, E. W., & Pearl, D. K. (1983). Time of conscious intention to act in relation to onset of cerebral activity (readiness-potential): The unconscious initiation of a freely voluntary act. *Brain, 106*(3), 623–642. http://doi.org/10.1093/brain/106.3.623.

Lieberman, D. A. (1997). Interactive video games for health promotion: Effects on knowledge, self-efficacy, social support, and health. In R. L. Street, W. R. Gold, & T. Manning (eds.), *Health promotion and interactive technology: Theoretical applications and future directions* (pp. 103–120). Mahwah, NJ: Lawrence Erlbaum Associates.

Lieberman, D. A. (2001a). Management of chronic pediatric diseases with interactive health games: Theory and research findings. *Journal of Ambulatory Care Management, 24*(1), 26–38.

Lieberman, D. A. (2001b). Using interactive media in communication campaigns for children and adolescents. In R. E. Rice & C. K. Atkin (eds.), *Public communication campaigns* (3rd ed., pp. 373–388). Thousand Oaks, CA: Sage.

Liu, L., Yao, Y.-W., Li, C.-S. R., Zhang, J.-T., Xia, C.-C., Lan, J., . . . Fang, X.-Y. (2018). The comorbidity between internet gaming disorder and depression: Interrelationship and neural mechanisms. *Frontiers in Psychiatry, 9*, 154. http://doi.org/10.3389/fpsyt.2018.00154.

Liu, Y., Teng, Z., Lan, H., Zhang, X., & Yao, D. (2015). Short-term effects of prosocial video games on aggression: An event-related potential study. *Frontiers in Behavioral Neuroscience, 9*, 12. Retrieved from https://search .proquest.com/docview/1817570742?accountid=10906; https://iastate .alma.exlibrisgroup.com/view/uresolver/01IASU_INST/openurl?url_ver =Z39.88-2004&rft_val_fmt=info:ofi/fmt:kev:mtx:journal&genre =article&sid=ProQ:ProQ%3Apsycinfo&atitle=Short-term+effects+of+pro social+video+games+on+aggression%3A+An+event-related+potential +study&title=Frontiers+in+Behavioral+Neuroscience&issn=1662– 5153&date=2015–07–24&volume=9&issue=&spage=äLiu%2C+Yanling %3BTeng%2C+Zhaojun%3BLan%2C+Haiying%3BZhang%2C+Xin% 3BYao%2C+Dezhong&isbn=&jtitle=Frontiers+in+Behavioral +Neuroscience&btitle=&rft_id=info:eric/2016–21023–001&rft_id=info: doi/.

Loftus, E. F. (1992). When a lie becomes memory's truth: Memory distortion after exposure to misinformation. *Current Directions in Psychological Science, 1*(4), 121–123.

Lynch, T., Tompkins, J. E., van Driel, I. I., & Fritz, N. (2016). Sexy, strong, and secondary: A content analysis of female characters in video games across 31 years. *Journal of Communication, 66*(4), 564–584. http://doi.org/10.1111 /jcom.12237.

Macnamara, B. N., Hambrick, D. Z., & Oswald, F. L. (2014). Deliberate practice and performance in music, games, sports, education, and professions: A meta-analysis. *Psychological Science, 25*(8), 1608–1618.

Maher, C. (2019). Video game sales to be just shy of $150 billion in 2019. Retrieved from www.vg247.com/2019/11/24/video-game-sales -150-billion-2019/#:~:text=Earlier%20this%20year%20it%20was,figure %20has%20recently%20been%20amended.

Maier, J. A. & Gentile, D. A. (2012). Learning aggression through the media: Comparing psychological and communication approaches. In L. J. Shrum (ed.), *The psychology of entertainment media: Blurring the lines between entertainment and persuasion* (2nd ed., pp. 267–299). New York: Taylor & Francis.

Markey, P. M. & Ferguson, C. J. (2017a). Internet gaming addiction: Disorder or moral panic? *American Journal of Psychiatry, 174*(3), 195–196. http://doi.org/10.1176/appi.ajp.2016.16121341.

Markey, P. M. & Ferguson, C. J. (2017b). Teaching us to fear: The violent video game moral panic and the politics of game research. *American Journal of Play, 10*(1), 99–115.

Mihara, S. & Higuchi, S. (2017). Cross-sectional and longitudinal epidemiological studies of internet gaming disorder: A systematic review of the literature. *Psychiatry and Clinical Neurosciences, 71*(7), 425–444. http://doi.org/10.1111/pcn.12532.

Miller, G. A. (1956). The magical number seven, plus or minus two: Some limits on our capacity for processing information. *Psychological Review, 63*(2), 81–97. http://doi.org/10.1037/h0043158.

Mullin, C. R. & Linz, D. (1995). Desensitization and resensitization to violence against women: Effects of exposure to sexually violent films on judgements of domestic violent victims. *Journal of Personality and Social Psychology, 69*, 449–459.

National Institute on Mental Health. (1982). *Television and behavior: Ten years of scientific progress and implications for the eighties* (Vol. 1). Washington, DC: US Government Printing Office.

Neisser, U. (1967). *Cognitive psychology.* New York: Appleton-Century-Crofts.

Ophir, E., Nass, C., & Wagner, A. D. (2009). Cognitive control in media multitaskers. *Proceedings of the National Academy of Sciences, 106*, 15583–15587.

Paik, H. & Comstock, G. (1994). The effects of television violence on antisocial behavior – A meta-analysis. *Communication Research, 21*, 516–546.

Paivio, A. (1991). Dual coding theory: Retrospect and current status. *Canadian Journal of Psychology/Revue canadienne de psychologie, 45*(3), 255.

Pavlov, I. P. (1927). *Conditioned reflexes: An investigation of the physiological activity of the cerebral cortex.* Oxford: Oxford University Press.

Pearl, D. (1982a). *Television and behavior: Ten years of scientific progress and implications for the eighties* (Volume II: Technical Reviews). Rockville, MD: National Institute of Mental Health.

Pearl, D. (1982b). *Television and behavior: Ten years of scientific progress and implications for the eighties* (Volume 1: Summary Report). Rockville, MD: National Institute of Mental Health.

Perry, L. K., Samuelson, L. K., Malloy, L. M., & Schiffer, R. N. (2010). Learn locally, think globally: Exemplar variability supports higher-order generalization and word learning. *Psychological Science, 21*(12), 1894–1902.

Plante, C., Anderson, C. A., Allen, J., Groves, C. L., & Gentile, D. A. (2020). *Game on! Sensible answers about video games and media violence.* Ames, IA: Zengen LLC.

Pope, Z., Zeng, N., & Gao, Z. (2017). The effects of active video games on patients' rehabilitative outcomes: A meta-analysis. *Preventive Medicine, 95*, 38–46. http://doi.org/10.1016/j.ypmed.2016.12.003.

Postman, L. (1962). Retention as a function of degree of overlearning. *Science, 135*, 666–667. http://doi.org/10.1126/science.135.3504.666.

Pressley, M., Borkowski, J. G., & O'Sullivan, J. T. (1984). Memory strategy instruction is made of this: Metamemory and durable strategy use. *Educational Psychologist, 19*(2), 94–107.

Prot, S. & Gentile, D. A. (2014). Applying risk and resilience models to predicting the effects of media violence on development. *Advances in Child Development and Behavior, 46*, 215–244.

Prot, S., Gentile, D. A., Anderson, C. A., Suzuki, K., Swing, E., Lim, K. M., . . . Lam, B. C. P. (2014). Long-term relations among prosocial-media use, empathy, and prosocial behavior. *Psychological Science, 25*(2), 358–368. http://doi.org/10.1177/0956797613503854.

Rakison, D. H. & Yermolayeva, Y. (2011). How to identify a domain-general learning mechanism when you see one. *Journal of Cognition and Development, 12*(2), 134–153.

Ratan, R. & Sah, Y. J. (2015). Leveling up on stereotype threat: The role of avatar customization and avatar embodiment. *Computers in Human Behavior, 50*, 367–374.

Ratan, R., Shen, C., & Williams, D. (2020). Men do not rule the world of tanks: Negating the gender-performance gap in a spatial-action game by controlling for time played. *American Behavioral Scientist, 64*(7), 1031–1043. http://doi.org/10.1177/0002764220919147.

Razran, G. (1949). Stimulus generalization of conditioned responses. *Psychological Bulletin, 46*(5), 337–365. http://doi.org/10.1037/h0060507.

Reynolds, J. H. & Glaser, R. (1964). Effects of repetition and spaced review upon retention of a complex learning task. *Journal of Educational Psychology, 55*(5), 297.

Rideout, V. J., Foehr, U. G., & Roberts, D. F. (2010). *Generation M²: Media in the lives of 8- to 18-year-olds.* Menlo Park, CA: Kaiser Family Foundation.

Rideout, V. J. & Robb, M. B. (2019). *The common sense census: Media use by tweens and teens.*San Francisco, CA: Common Sense Media.

Rokkum, J. N. & Gentile, D. A. (2018). Primary versus secondary disorder in the context of internet gaming disorder. *Current Addiction Reports, 5*(4), 485–490. http://doi.org/10.1007/s40429-018-0222-y.

Rosser, J. C., Gentile, D. A., Hanigan, K., & Danner, O. K. (2012). The effect of video game "warm-up" on performance of laparoscopic surgery tasks. *Journal of the Society of Laparoendoscopic Surgeons, 16*, 3–9.

Rosser, J. C., Lynch, P. J., Cuddihy, L., Gentile, D. A., Klonsky, J., & Merrell, R. (2007). The impact of video games on training surgeons in the 21st century. *Archives of Surgery, 142*, 181–186. http://doi.org/142/2/181 [pii]10.1001/archsurg.142.2.181.

Rothman, A. J. & Hardin, C. D. (1997). Differential use of the availability heuristic in social judgment. *Personality and Social Psychology Bulletin, 23* (2), 123–138. http://doi.org/10.1177/0146167297232002.

Ruth, N. (2016). "Heal the world": A field experiment on the effects of music with prosocial lyrics on prosocial behavior. *Psychology of Music, 45*(2), 298–304. http://doi.org/10.1177/0305735616652226.

Ryan, R. M. & Deci, E. L. (2000). The darker and brighter sides of human existence: Basic psychological needs as a unifying concept. *Psychological Inquiry, 11*(4), 319–338.

Ryan, R. M., Rigby, C. S., & Przybylski, A. (2006). The motivational pull of video games: A self-determination theory approach. *Motivation and Emotion, 30*, 347–363.

Saleem, M. & Anderson, C. A. (2013). Arabs as terrorists: Effects of stereotypes within violent contexts on attitudes, perceptions, and affect. *Psychology of Violence, 3*(1), 84–99. http://doi.org/10.1037/a0030038.

Saleem, M., Anderson, C. A., & Gentile, D. A. (2012a). Effects of prosocial, neutral, and violent video games on children's helpful and hurtful behaviors. *Aggressive Behavior, 38*(4), 281–287. http://doi.org/10.1002/ab.21428.

Saleem, M., Anderson, C. A., & Gentile, D. A. (2012b). Effects of prosocial, neutral, and violent video games on college students' affect. *Aggressive Behavior, 38*(4), 263–271. http://doi.org/10.1002/ab.21427.

Saleem, M., Barlett, C. P., Anderson, C. A., & Hawkins, I. (2017). Helping and hurting others: Person and situation effects on aggressive and prosocial behavior as assessed by the Tangram task. *Aggressive Behavior, 43*(2), 133–146.

Saleem, M., Prot, S., Anderson, C. A., & Lemieux, A. F. (2017). Exposure to Muslims in media and support for public policies harming Muslims. *Communication Research, 44*(6), 841–869.

Salomon, G. & Perkins, D. N. (1989). Rocky roads to transfer: Rethinking the mechanism of a neglected phenomenon. *Educational Psychologist, 24*(2), 113–142.

Savage, J. & Yancey, C. (2008). The effects of media violence exposure on criminal aggression: A meta-analysis. *Criminal Justice and Behavior, 35,* 772–791.

Schwarz, N., Bless, H., Strack, F., Klumpp, G., Rittenauer-Schatka, H., & Simons, A. (1991). Ease of retrieval as information: Another look at the availability heuristic. *Journal of Personality and Social Psychology, 61*(2), 195–202. http://doi.org/10.1037/0022-3514.61.2.195.

Seligman, M. E. P. (1974). *Depression and learned helplessness.* Washington: John Wiley.

Seligman, M. E. P. (1975). *Helplessness: On depression, development, and death. A series of books in psychology.* New York: WH Freeman/Times Books/Henry Holt.

Selod, S. (2015). Citizenship denied: The racialization of Muslim American men and women post-9/11. *Critical Sociology, 41*(1), 77–95. http://doi.org /10.1177/0896920513516022.

Sherry, J. L. (2001). The effects of violent video games on aggression. *Human Communication Research, 27,* 409–431.

Shuell, T. J. (1969). Clustering and organization in free recall. *Psychological Bulletin, 72*(5), 353.

Sidman, M. (1960). Normal sources of pathological behavior. *Science, 132* (3419), 61–68. http://doi.org/10.1126/science.132.3419.61.

Siegel, J. M. (2001). The REM sleep-memory consolidation hypothesis. *Science, 294*(5544), 1058–1063.

Singley, M. K. & Anderson, J. R. (1989). *The transfer of cognitive skill.* Cambridge, MA: Harvard University Press.

Skinner, B. F. (1938). *Behavior of organisms.* New York: Appleton-Century-Crofts.

Skinner, B. F. (1974). *About behaviorism.* New York: Alfred A. Knopf.

Spencer, S. J., Steele, C. M., & Quinn, D. M. (1999). Stereotype threat and women's math performance. *Journal of Experimental Social Psychology, 35* (1), 4–28. http://doi.org/10.1006/jesp.1998.1373.

Statista Research Department. (2016). U.S. computer and video game sales from 2000 to 2015. Retrieved from www.statista.com/statistics/273258/us-computer-and-video-game-sales/.

Subcommittee on Youth Violence. (2013). *Youth violence: What we need to know.* Washington, DC: National Science Foundation.

Subrahmanyam, K. & Greenfield, P. M. (1994). Effect of video game practice on spatial skills in girls and boys. *Journal of Applied Developmental Psychology, 15*(1), 13–32. http://doi.org/10.1016/0193-3973(94)90004-3.

Swing, E. L. & Anderson, C. A. (2014). The role of attention problems and impulsiveness in media violence effects on aggression. *Aggressive Behavior, 40*(3), 197–203. http://doi.org/10.1002/ab.21519.

Swing, E. L., Gentile, D. A., Anderson, C. A., & Walsh, D. A. (2010). Television and video game exposure and the development of attention problems. *Pediatrics, 126,* 214–221. http://doi.org/10.1542/peds.2009-1508.

Teasdale, J. D. & Russell, M. L. (1983). Differential effects of induced mood on the recall of positive, negative and neutral words. *British Journal of Clinical Psychology, 22*(3), 163–171.

Thorndike, E. L. (1911). *Animal intelligence: Experimental studies.* New York, Hafner: Forgotten Books.

Thorndike, E. L. (1923). The influence of first-year Latin upon ability to read english. *School & Society, 17,* 165–168.

Thorndike, E. L. & Woodworth, R. S. (1901). The influence of improvement in one mental function upon the efficiency of other functions. II. The estimation of magnitudes. *Psychological Review, 8*(4), 384.

Tolman, E. C. (1932). *Purposive behavior in animals and men.* New York: Century.

Tolman, E. C. (1959). Principles of purposive behavior. *Psychology: A Study of a Science, 2,* 92–157.

Tulving, E. (1962). The effect of alphabetical subjective organization on memorizing unrelated words. *Canadian Journal of Psychology/Revue canadienne de psychologie, 16*(3), 185.

Tulving, E. & Psotka, J. (1971). Retroactive inhibition in free recall: Inaccessibility of information available in the memory store. *Journal of Experimental Psychology, 87*(1), 1.

Tulving, E. & Thomson, D. M. (1973). Encoding specificity and retrieval processes in episodic memory. *Psychological Review, 80*(5), 352–373.

Underwood, B. J. (1954). Speed of learning and amount retained: A consideration of methodology. *Psychological Bulletin, 51*(3), 276.

Underwood, B. J. (1957). Interference and forgetting. *Psychological Review, 64* (1), 49.

US Surgeon General. (2001). *Youth violence: A report of the surgeon general.* Washington, DC: United States Surgeon General.

Walker, M. P. & Stickgold, R. (2004). Sleep-dependent learning and memory consolidation. *Neuron, 44*(1), 121–133. http://doi.org/10.1016/j.neuron.2004.08.031.

Walsh, D. A. & Gentile, D. A. (2001). A validity test of movie, television, and video-game ratings. *Pediatrics, 107*(6), 1302–1308. http://doi.org/10.1542/peds.107.6.1302.

Warren, R. M. & Warren, R. P. (1970). Auditory illusions and confusions. *Scientific American, 223*(6), 30–37.

Wartberg, L., Kriston, L., Zieglmeier, M., Lincoln, T., & Kammerl, R. (2019). A longitudinal study on psychosocial causes and consequences of internet gaming disorder in adolescence. *Psychological Medicine, 49*(2), 287–294. http://doi.org/10.1017/s003329171800082x.

Watson, J. B. (1913). Psychology as the behaviorist views it. *Psychological Review, 20*(2), 158–177.

Watson, J. B. (1919). *Psychology from the standpoint of a behaviorist.* Philadelphia, PA: J. B. Lippincott.

Watson, J. B. & Rayner, R. (1920). Conditioned emotional responses. *Journal of Experimental Psychology, 3*(1), 1–14.

Weiner, B. (1974). *Achievement motivation and attribution theory.* Morristown, NJ: General Learning Press.

Weiner, B. (2010). The development of an attribution-based theory of motivation: A history of ideas. *Educational Psychologist, 45*(1), 28–36.

Willingham, D. T. (2004). Ask the cognitive scientist practice makes perfect, but only if you practice beyond the point of perfection. *American Educator, 28*(1), 31–33.

World Health Organization. (April 2019). ICD-11 for mortality and morbidity statistics: 6C51 gaming disorder. Retrieved from https://icd.who.int/browse11/l-m/en#/http://id.who.int/icd/entity/1448597234.

Xu, W., Liang, H.-N., Baghaei, N., Wu Berberich, B., & Yue, Y. (2020). Health benefits of digital videogames for the aging population: A systematic review. *Games for Health Journal, 9*, 389–404.

Yao, M. Z., Mahood, C., & Linz, D. (2010). Sexual priming, gender stereotyping, and likelihood to sexually harass: Examining the cognitive effects of playing a sexually-explicit video game. *Sex Roles, 62*(1–2), 77–88. http://doi.org/10.1007/s11199-009-9695-4.

Yee, N. (2001). *The Norrathian scrolls: A study of EverQuest (Version 2.5).* Retrieved from www.nickyee.com/eqt/report.html.

Zajonc, R. B. (1980). Feeling and thinking: Preferences need no inferences. *American Psychologist, 35*(2), 151–175. http://doi.org/10.1037/0003-066X .35.2.151.

Zajonc, R. B. (1984). On the primacy of affect. *American Psychologist, 39*(2), 117–123. http://doi.org/10.1037/0003-066X.39.2.117.

Cambridge Elements ≡

Applied Social Psychology

Susan Clayton
College of Wooster, Ohio

Susan Clayton is a social psychologist at the College of Wooster in Wooster, Ohio. Her research focuses on the human relationship with nature, how it is socially constructed, and how it can be utilized to promote environmental concern.

Editorial Board

About the Series

Many social psychologists have used their research to understand and address pressing social issues, from poverty and prejudice to work and health. Each Element in this series reviews a particular area of applied social psychology. Elements will also discuss applications of the research findings and describe directions for future study.

Cambridge Elements ≡

Applied Social Psychology

Elements in the Series

Empathy and Concern with Negative Evaluation in Intergroup Relations: Implications for Designing Effective Interventions
Jacquie D. Vorauer

The Psychology of Climate Change Adaptation
Anne van Valkengoed and Linda Steg

Undoing the Gender Binary
Charlotte Chucky Tate, Ella Ben Hagai and Faye J. Crosby

Selves as Solutions to Social Inequalities: Why Engaging the Full Complexity of Social Identities is Critical to Addressing Disparities
Tiffany N. Brannon, Peter H. Fisher and Abigail J. Greydanus

Identity Development During STEM Integration for Underrepresented Minority Students
Sophie L. Kuchynka, Alexander E. Gates and Luis M. Rivera

The Psychology of Effective Activism
Robyn Gulliver, Susilo Wibisono, Kelly S. Fielding and Winnifred R. Louis

Learning from Video Games (and Everything Else): The General Learning Model
Douglas A. Gentile and J. Ronald Gentile

A full series listing is available at: www.cambridge.org/EASP

Printed in the United States
by Baker & Taylor Publisher Services